Sympathy for Jonah

Sympathy
for Jonah

Reflections on Humiliation, Terror
and the Politics of Enemy-Love

David Benjamin Blower

foreword by
Ched Myers

RESOURCE *Publications* · Eugene, Oregon

Resource Publications
An Imprint of Wipf and Stock Publishers
199 W. 8th Ave., Suite 3
Eugene, OR 97401

www.wipfandstock.com

PAPERBACK ISBN: 978-1-4982-3727-7
HARDCOVER ISBN: 978-1-4982-3729-1
EBOOK ISBN: 978-1-4982-3728-4

Manufactured in the U.S.A.   JULY 7, 2016

For Kate, Jesse-John & Rosa

Contents

Foreword

by Ched Myers

"This evil generation seeks a sign, but none shall be given to it except the sign of Jonah." —Luke 11:29

DAVID BENJAMIN BLOWER'S LITTLE book on the little book of Jonah—and don't be fooled by the adjective in either case—begins as an exploration of the biblical tall tale as sea shanty, then as musical both comic and tragic. Along the way the Birmingham musician (and performance artist, activist and theologian) manages to liberate Jonah from scholarly shrugs and Sunday School trivialization, not to mention from racist and anti-Semitic hermeneutics.

Both church folk who treat the Jonah narrative as mere morality tale or children's entertainment, and academics intent on dehistoricizing it, have utterly missed what Blower calls its radical "Interruption" of imperial history and its political orthodoxies. He puts it succinctly: "The grace of God is awful to us, because the proper response to evil is to fear it and desire its destruction not to love it and desire its redemption." Make no mistake: this ethos revealed in Jonah poses a challenge to our credulity far more profound than does a magical whale tale.

To undomesticate this fable, Blower rightly recontextualizes it in terms of the awful violence of the Assyrian empire, which he analogizes as an ancient Nazi regime. Indeed, the Assyrian capital of Nineveh was so infamous in the consciousness of biblical Israel that it merits special mention in the "genealogy of empire" that culminates the primeval Creation/Fall story (Gen 10:11f). And it earns ample prophetic antipathy, particularly in the oracles of Nahum and Zephaniah, which though even shorter than Jonah, spare no disdain for the Assyrian conquerors.

"Woe to the bloody city, all full of lies and booty—no end to the plunder!" rants Nahum. His ensuing portrait of Assyria's violent militarism—of which Israel was on the receiving end—is dramatic and poignant, but hardly exaggerated:

> The crack of whip, and rumble of wheel, galloping horse and bounding chariot! Horsemen charging, flashing sword and glittering spear, hosts of slain, heaps of corpses, dead bodies without end—they stumble over the bodies![1]

Similarly, Zephaniah longed for the day in which Yahweh would

> destroy Assyria; and make Nineveh a desolation, a dry waste like the desert . . . This is the exultant city that dwelt secure, that said to herself, "I am and there is none else." What a desolation she has become, a lair for wild beasts! Everyone who passes by her hisses and shakes his fist.[2]

For people who have been brutalized by imperial presumption and aggression, ancient or modern, such bitter lament and vengeful hopes for destruction can surely be understood.

Which is what makes the book of Jonah such a curious (if admittedly reluctant) counterpoint. The divine assignment here is not to eliminate the adversary, but to turn them around. This is "a call so terrible," Blower acknowledges, "that even when the story's curtain falls the protagonist still cannot accept it." Perhaps even more extraordinary is the story's imagination that Nineveh might actually repent! The portrait of King Sennacharib (think Hitler) in sackcloth, in my opinion, was meant as a political cartoon, skewering at once both the empire and the prophet. As Blower recognizes, such self-deprecating satire is common in the Hebrew

---

1. Nahum 3:1–3
2. Zephaniah 2:13, 15

Bible (though unique in the literature of antiquity). But this trope, however fantastic, underlines the fact that ultimately, if humanity is to survive, the murderous logic of empire *must be turned around*. And nothing less is God's will for history.

This appears to be the lesson that Jesus drew from the old prophetic tale, as he took up John's proclamation of repentance after the Baptist was disappeared in an imperial prison. "For as Jonah became a sign to the people of Nineveh," the Nazarene warns in Luke 11:30, "so will the Human One be to this generation." "I can't think of any person or character in history or fiction," writes Blower, "who seemed so completely bent on the Jonaic practice."

Christian theology has, as Blower points out multiple times, both overlooked and underestimated the Jonah story, on its own terms and as a kind of interpretive key to the Jesus story. Both stories culminate at a tree, the Cross revealing what was implicit under the branches of Jonah's broom: namely, that only the loving power of a nonviolent resistance that seeks to redeem the oppressor can defy and dismantle the evils of empire, then and now.

I commend this brilliant reading of one of the Bible's most mishandled texts. Full of theological, psychological and political insight, it faithfully re-presents the scandal of both Jonah and Jesus. Now, brother Benjamin, I await the musical!

Acknowledgments

My thanks go to Ched Myers and Jonathan Blower for their invaluable suggestions and contributions to this little book. I also beg the indulgence of the reader regarding the many footnotes in it, since, try as I might, I could not get it to go in a straight line.

Introduction

The Fisherman's Tale & the Tomb

IF I DID GO around for a while, like a man telling tall tales, assuring people that I had written a musical of the book of Jonah, it was not with the intention of misleading anyone. I exaggerated, to be sure; partly because it is, after all, a fisherman's tale and exaggeration feels quite natural to it, and partly because I didn't know what else to call it.

As I tried to explain the thing to a friend, he told me frankly that it was a reading of the Book of Jonah, with some songs popping up here and there. I must say that this description dissatisfied me. One cannot contemplate the story of Jonah without a touch of theatre. We would wear hats and eye patches and sack-cloth. We'd light candles for the sailor's vows, and we'd recreate the whale's belly using a red torch.

No doubt, this little project sprang partly from the Englishman's usual fascination with maritime lore, sea-monsters and ancient cities and civilizations. But if there was any frivolity involved, a little time spent with the prophet Jonah would soon cure me of that. And yet I had no idea how deep and dark Jonah's well would eventually turn out to be, or how unanswerable the questions he would ask.

As I was pulling these songs together in the summer of 2014, some very dark stories were beginning to go around about happenings in northern Iraq. And then one day, I saw a short video of a mosque being blown into a flameless puff of gray dust. I read that this mosque was said to house the shrine of the prophet Jonah along with a whale's tooth—according to both Islamic tradition and to the Church of the East—and that it had been blown up by Islamic State militants who considered it to be idolatrous, and who were busy erasing any history and cultural heritage that had preceded the great new civilization they believed themselves to be bringing. From here on the stories from the land of Nineveh only became darker and darker still. So much so that, for a while, I lost all appetite for playing the songs I'd written.

For Jonah himself—who has a miserable time in his own story, a most unforgiving write-up from many commentators, and whose name is, to this day, synonymous with *bad luck* among sea-faring people—this is business as usual. And it is, I should think, ridiculous to waste too much sadness on the alleged tombs of long-dead prophets in the face of all that is currently going on in Iraq and Syria. But the more I dwelt on this web of horrible stories the more I began to see a poetic tragedy in the maritime prophet being dragged into them, and also a poetic hope—though only by way of a journey that neither he, nor I, nor you dear reader, if you have any sense at all, would wish to take.

The Whale

On my first encounter with Jonah's hell ~ On the ubiquity of the myth ~ On the image as a psychological archetype ~ On the monster as providence and grace ~ On rebirth ~ On the necessity of humility to understand humiliation and the necessity of humiliation to precede revolution

I HAVE, AT THE time of writing, performed just a few scrappy run-throughs of our musical retelling of the Book of Jonah, in a few lounges and to a handful of friends. Some have commented that the whale doesn't play as big a part as might be expected. For most of us the whale is probably the story's second character, if not the first. And for myself, like almost everybody else, it was Jonah's encounter with the whale, or rather the "great fish," that first pulled me into the story.

It happened one summer's night that I was to play a local bar. But I was in strange moods at the time, one of the milder symptoms being that I was sick of my own music and wanting to play something else. Michael, who plays the accordion, suggested playing a set of sea shanties and it seemed good to me. Among other things we played a song by The Decemberists about a showdown between two enemies who find themselves face to face having been swallowed by the same whale. And of course we played the lord of all existential sea shanties "Starving in the Belly of a Whale" by Tom Waits. We also had readings from *Moby Dick* about the murderous albino whale, and from the second chapter of the Book of Jonah which recounts the prophet's prayer from the belly of the whale. There are songs and tales of the sea that do not involve whale ingestion but it seems we were only drawn to those that did.

Being of fragile mind at the time, I found reading Jonah's prayer from inside the fish, all set to Michael's miserable squeezebox dirge, crushing, horrible and unbearable. The imagery of being thrown into a raging ocean—which rages for you and you alone—and sinking down to a cold, dark, wet, airless death, away from all human pity, drowning in your own fault, only then to encounter the gaping mouth of some unknowable monster with vacant eyes approaching from the black salt oblivion; this is a meditation that falls beneath nihilistic terror. The words which follow from Jonah's prayer are as vividly hellish as children's nightmares. I felt my innards turn cold and hard as they sometimes did in that strange season, swallowed alive by this psalm of doom.

Then we played "Troublesome Waters" by Johnny Cash which has no whales in it, and I began to recover myself. What is it about the extraordinary thought of being swallowed by a whale that seems so awful and yet so tangible to the imagination?

The Book of Jonah is very short. It takes up less than two pages of any Bible. But still everybody knows who Jonah is. A lot of pious Christians can't tell you anything about Amos or Haggai or Micah or Ezekiel, but even if you ask the secularites about Jonah, most of them will tell you, he's the man who was swallowed by a whale, just as he is known in Islam as "the man of the fish."[1] This short and bizarre tale at the back end of the Hebrew Bible has become ubiquitous legend, filed away in everybody's mind. It's probably true that most of us have not got much idea what the book is actually about. The fact that it's a recognizable myth, even in the days of secular disenchantment, I should think lies simply in the incredible power of that image: the person swallowed by a whale.[2]

---

1. Sura 21:87.

2. Variations of the image crop up all over the place: the biblical image of

Let's imagine the story of Jonah goes like this: God tells the prophet to go to Nineveh but the prophet takes flight instead, joining a Bedouin tribe as they head south. After many days the whole tribe has caught some terrible illness and divined that Jonah is the cause of their misfortune. They agree with much reluctance—for they have grown fond of the prophet—to expel him into the desert where he faces a sandy death. Then, unexpectedly, the wandering and dying Jonah is hoisted onto the back of an African elephant (who is lost) and carried the three days elephant-march back to where he had begun; and there God reiterates his commission to the prophet, and so on. The plot is the same, but would the story hold such mythical power if it happened this way? Would we all know who Jonah was, or would he have been as obscure to most of us as Balaam and his talking ass or Elisha, who calls the wrath of an angry bear to his aid? Why must it be a whale to stick in the mind?

Perhaps it has something to do with the mysterious structures of the mind. "How else," wrote Carl Jung,

> Could it have occurred to man to divide the cosmos [. . .] into a bright day-world and a dark night-world peopled with fabulous monsters, unless he had the prototype of such a division in himself, in the polarity between the conscious and the invisible and unknowable unconscious?[3]

Can anyone who is not entirely insensible to the chaos under the floorboards of their own mind escape the psychological metaphor of the ocean surface as the boundary that divides the known world from the unknown, where wild things swim past our feet in the

---

Leviathan, the maritime legend of the Kraken, the Greek myth of Heracles, who was eaten by a sea monster and killed it by hacking his way out again, and Andromeda, who was offered to another one sent from Hades. Jules Verne's *Twenty Thousand Leagues Under the Sea*, Spielberg's *Jaws* and its *terra firma* counterpart, the marvelous B movie *Tremors* (giant man-eating worms rumbling underfoot in Texas), *Pinocchio*, *The Adventures of Baron Münchhausen*, the young black Bob Dylan in the film *I'm not there*. And any number of others you can think of.

3. Jung, *Four Archetypes*, 38.

murky depths, terrifying not because we can see them but because we can't?[4] Perhaps we feel we know something of Jonah's whale because we sense in it some resonance with our own forgotten nightmares, formless thoughts, and the unresolved troubles that glide darkly beneath us.

It would of course be ridiculous and typical of the present age to talk about the Book of Jonah as though it were written as a sort of psychological exploration of this kind. I hope it will be understood that I'm not wanting to make suggestions here regarding what the Book of Jonah is about (not yet anyway), but I do think perhaps Jonah's whale casts its own gloomy light on what we human beings are about. Why is the image of a man on his knees in the belly of a whale so compelling to us? The imagery seems to sit in our collective mind precisely because it gives us an archetypal image that resounds with the inner experiences of the human being. I will dare to hope that its psychological resonance might in the end help us to understand what the Book of Jonah really is about, and illuminate the meaning of its terrible call. But we may at least start with the fact that this is, after all, a book about a man who runs from his issues and ends up confronting them on his knees in the warm, wet hell of the monster's belly. He undergoes a night sea journey, a dark night of the soul. And it is thought by some that all of us must either embark on such a journey and be changed by it, or else barricade our entire lives against its cruel interruption.

---

4. It is impossible here not to think of what might be the most iconic film poster of the last century. I have always been disturbed by Roger Kastel's image for Steven Spielberg's *Jaws*, with its monstrously oversized shark that could have swallowed a car, racing upward towards a hapless swimmer. Apart from Hollywood's usual fascination with violence against the sexualized bodies of women, something about the trajectory of the shark's approach has always made an impression on me. Since the shark is the size of a blue whale and is swimming directly upwards for the kill, how deep is the water? It seemed to my mind to go down forever. No doubt the power of the image lies in its metaphorical suggestion of those two worlds of light and darkness—one all-knowing and terrible, and the other merrily oblivious—separated by the thin film of the water's surface.

So for these sorts of reasons our reflections begin not with chapter one of the book, but chapter two, in the darkness and chaos where,

> The waters compassed me about, even to the soul: the depths closed me round about, the weeds were wrapped about my head. I went to the bottoms of the mountains: the earth with her bars was about me forever.[5]

I doubt that any deeper dungeon has been described outside of Dante's hell, but it is the utter loneliness of the image that turns the blood cold. At least *The Inferno* received visitors. When thinking too hard on Jonah's descent I find my sorry way back to a boyhood fear of being buried alive, or of being lost to some hateful nothingness that has no end. The image isn't nihilistic. The terror of it lies in his having been willfully discarded into it, abandoned to it, by the hand of his maker; in slipping through the cracks of love into oblivion: "Thou hadst cast me into the deep, in the midst of the seas: and the floods compassed me about; all thy billows and thy waves passed over me."[6]

And what to make of the great fish? The image by itself carries with it a sense of fatedness, of doom or inevitability; as though the monster had been swimming around looking for Jonah all of

---

5. Jonah 2:5–6.

6. Jonah 2:3. I have always been told that, in Jewish thought, the ocean is to be associated with chaos and evil and such. It's where Jesus sends demonized pigs, where dragons emerge and where leviathan lives, and when everything is made new there will be no sea (alas for the resurrected mariners). But the image seems to me ambiguous, not least in the Book of Jonah. Whether or not chaos and evil are the same thing, I don't know. That rare breed of creation scientists are ever at pains to say that the void formlessness of the earth at the beginning of the Genesis story has nothing of evil about it, nor the sea which covers everything, and the leviathan which thrashes therein may be the enemy of men and women, but not of God, as evil is. Rather, God is leviathan's lord and master, which is a relationship that echoes through Jesus' stern words to the choppy sea of Galilee and his playful way of walking on it. The sea doesn't seem to evoke God's wrath as Babylon does. Rather it is a god which must be tamed for the sake of humanity, because, evil or not, it has been a thing of terror to men and women—much like the obscure underside of the mind—and into the hands of this terror Jonah must go.

its cold, gray life. But the beast which Jonah calls "hell" is not described by the narrator in the language of judgment, but of providence and grace; the grace that comes in the form of unspeakable terror, if we dare believe in such a thing. Once past the teeth and through the gullet, perhaps many of us might even feel a sort of warming solace about that dark belly which God had "prepared" for him under those hospitably arched ribs. Such is the hopeful glow that Pinocchio discovers when he finds, deep in the shark's belly, his maker Old Joe bleached white and sat at a rotten old table burning the last candle from some swallowed shipwreck. In this melancholy meeting the wooden boy finally lets spill the whole tale of his trials and woes.[7] And it is in the sea monster's innards that Baron Münchhausen is reunited with the old comrades who will help him to fulfill his future purpose. Somehow many have sensed a certain warmth toward the strange monster that rescues Jonah from the chaos of the sea and holds him in against the storm and carries him like a child in the comfort of irresponsibility.[8] Here,

---

7. Collodi, *Pinocchio*, 153-55.

8. In his essay "Inside the Whale" George Orwell talks of the belly of the fish as a wonderful place of total passivity, a womb for an adult where one need not be concerned with anything. His metaphor refers to those writers who resist the heated (and scripted) political debates of their day and are able to continue writing simply about the mirth and the pathos of the human condition while Rome burns. They seem on one hand apathetic, but in their defense, perhaps they show that the political dialectics of the day have become an ideological clamor that is itself apathetic to what it means to be human. In other words, the whale cures us of belonging to some political or ideological position, rather than to humanity itself. He's paraphrasing Henry Miller, who is thinking not of Jonah but of Anaïs Nin the nineteenth century writer of essays and short stories. However, the image is interesting to us for several reasons, which will become more obvious as we continue. See Orwell, *Inside the Whale*, 42-43.

Another vision of the whale's benevolence comes to us from a rabbinic text of the medieval period, *Pirke de Rabbi Eliezer,* where Jonah takes on the ilk of a classical hero and the great fish becomes a vision of some primitive science fiction. Jonah is able to see through the eyes of the fish as if they were windows, and is taken to see the wonders under the sea, conversing with his carrier as he goes. Jonah even rescues his aquatic host from Leviathan who has threatened to eat him (or her). Jonah requests that the fish take him to confront Leviathan and then rebukes the monster by showing it the seal of Abraham and threatening to hook it through the tongue and roast it for the eschatological feast of the

when all vexatious choices and courses of action are out of reach, one can make peace with even a bad situation. The whale's belly creates the space where Jonah's flight from God—which is also his flight from himself—ends. Here is the safe place to collapse, to give up and to allow one's inner structures, defenses, boundaries and coping strategies to be relaxed, or even demolished, so that some new thought can be thought. It is the cave of melancholy council and the awful darkness where unexpected newness can begin. Here Jonah can pray. Here and here only, in hellish gloom, can Jonah speak of hopeful things:

> I'm cast out of thy sight: yet I will look again toward thy holy temple [. . .] When my soul fainted within me I remembered the Lord, and my prayer came in unto thee [. . .] I will sacrifice unto thee with a voice of thanksgiving.[9]

We will find that thankfulness is quite far from the prophet on much better days. It is in the belly of hell that his life seems to him to be something good, something to be thankful for. He concludes absurdly there in the bile and the blackness: "Salvation is of the Lord."[10]

And after three days he is vomited up onto the sand.

Jung describes the Jonah-and-the-whale image as one of rebirth, linking the whale's belly with the mother's womb, as psychoanalysts ever will. "How can a man be born when he is old?" asks one rabbi of another. "Can he enter the second time into his mother's womb, and be born?"[11] Jung, for one, says we can and we must, and we share a feeling for Jonah precisely because we know it to be true. We must experience darkness and weakness, failure and evil and come to terms with them if we are to do anything but skate over the surface of life. The whale is a rite of passage, an initiation

------

righteous at the end of the age. See Limburg, *Jonah*, 106-07.

9. Jonah 2:4, 7 & 9.

10. Jonah 2:9.

11. John 3:4.

into goodness-knows-what. "Unless a grain of wheat falls into the earth and dies, it remains alone; but if it dies, it bears much fruit," says Jesus, the other rabbi, who must also experience wilderness, hunger, dark thoughts and wild animals before he begins to lead his oddly successful movement, and who must also die before he can speak the new word of resurrection into the world.[12] And it is on this point exactly that he himself cites the archetypal Jonah image.[13]

There is a bizarre detail of the text here: the Hebrew for "great fish" switches from the masculine to the feminine at the end of Jonah's nautical journey, which makes it ever more difficult to avoid seeing this as a most alarming image of rebirth. When Jonah rolls out of the monster's mouth, a mucusy whelp sprawled on a Mediterranean beach, he was not simply back where he started, he was a new man of some sort. I doubt anyone could interpret his change in the vein of that crude caricature of a protestant conversion: from being a bad man to a good one, or a troubled man to a resolved one, or a hot-headed man to a subdued one. Rather, Jonah had finally begun to have out with himself the argument with himself that he had hitherto been running away from. His

---

12. John 12:24.

13. "Just as Jonah was three days and three nights in the great fish, so will the Son of Man be three days and three nights in the heart of the earth" says Jesus (Matthew 12:40). All this talk of water and death and Jesus might well lead us to ponder the rite of baptism where we are submerged underwater and into death in order to be reborn—that is, into Jesus' death, which he himself relates to Jonah's odyssey in the Whale. And so in baptism, if we allow ourselves to join the dots, we too must go down into the belly of the whale and learn what it has to teach us. The rite of baptism is also associated, not only with his death and resurrection (Romans 6:3), but also with his wilderness experience (Matthew 3:13-4:1) and his insistence on rebirth (John 3:3–5). Perhaps there is a danger of the rite being only a symbol that doesn't in the end find its radical and transformative reality in a person's life. Just as the narrator of *Moby Dick* paddles away from the floating wreckage in a coffin, and just as mutineers from the British empire's brutal trading ships flew the morbid sign of the Jolly Roger, the disciples were told that if they were to follow Jesus they would have to journey the rest of their lives carrying the deathly burden of a Roman cross. More on this later.

humiliation had *begun*, and perhaps it was the greatest thing that would ever happen to him.[14]

If we lack an acquaintance with humiliation ourselves, regarding the swirling pools of our own problems, we may be inclined, as so many have been, to interpret the whole episode something like this: Jonah was badly behaved so God sent a fish to scold him, or Jonah went the wrong way so God sent a fish to bring him back the right way. Not without some truth of course, but I would have thought there'd be more to it than that. Must we have such a fisherman's tale to make such an obvious point? And what a long way to go only to arrive back at the beginning! It would seem odd to spend the first half of such a short story merely ironing out a false start. To my mind the image is too potent to leave it there. Jesus certainly sees a more mysterious and counter-intuitive phenomenon at work in this archetypal image, as rabbis sometimes will. The deviation from the path is somehow found to be the path itself. The moment of humiliation is the moment of glory. The death of something is its beginning, and nothing can be begun without such a death. When he refers to Jonah's bane in the whale it is not in tune with the common idea that he was being chastised for a lack of Victorian missionary zeal, but rather with reference to his own anticipated humiliation and his descent into death, where "the earth with her bars was about me forever."[15] This was understood to be a glorious, redemptive and necessary journey that would

14. While the image of whale ingestion followed by escape usually seems to imply that the person is somehow changed, humbled and wizened by their encounter with the beast, a curious exception comes to us from the era of modernity, progress and the conquest of nature. Rudyard Kipling's tale of the seaman who is swallowed by a whale tells how the resourceful, inventive and irrepressible mariner made the whale that ate him so uncomfortable that he was able to dictate terms to it and be delivered to the nearest beach. But before he alighted he made a grate out of the wreckage of his raft and lodged it in the monster's throat to make sure he never swallowed anyone again. And that is how the whale got his throat. So it was thought to be the whale that was forever changed by its encounter with the irrepressible human spirit, not the other way around: a reversal most fitting for that rather optimistic and eccentric era of human history. See Kipling, *Just So Stories*, 25–28.

15. Jonah 2:6.

bring about resurrection, and a redemptive movement after itself. It's notable that Jonah's humiliation also precedes a story of revolution—albeit an unexpected one. God help the revolution that has not first known humiliation.

If we have underplayed the whale in our musical retelling, I suppose it's because the whale is the one thing everybody already knows about the story of Jonah. Why should I replace the image you already have in your mind with the one I have in mine, as Hollywood films are always so eager to do? I have a suspicion that the Book of Jonah is really about something much more than a man who was swallowed by a whale, but if we are to take note of that Jewish literary tradition of making the book's main statement at its center point, we will then at least find ourselves looking roughly at Jonah's slimy rebirth from the monstrous gullet. The question then becomes, from what was he being transformed, and for what purpose?

2

The Boat to Nowhere

On Jonah's flight and our lack of sympathy ~ The inability of pride to understand humiliation ~ Was Jonah racist? ~ On the anti-Semitism of Christian exegesis and religious parricide ~ On the folly of noticing the story's content but not its existence ~ Pascal on Jewish history ~ On the irony of Christian anti-Semitism and Jewish universalism

SINCE SHARING THE WHALE's belly with him that night I have come to feel a certain attachment to the prophet Jonah, and indeed when I think of the ways in which I've heard Christians speaking of the prophet I've become not only attached but also rather protective. He's not always recalled with much kindness, sympathy or understanding. To see what I mean we will now start the story from its beginning. It begins on dry land with a divine commission, which the prophet refuses:

> Now the word of the Lord came unto Jonah son of Amittai, saying, arise, go to Nineveh, that great city, and cry against it; for their wickedness is come up before me. But Jonah rose up to flee unto Tarshish from the presence of the Lord, and went down to Joppa; and he found a ship going to Tarshish: so he paid the fare thereof.[1]

1. Jonah 1:1–3.

11

And many theologians and commentators and such have written a great many pages asking the question, "why?" He is the only prophet in the Hebrew Bible to have ever turned a calling down. What was it about this job that was so distasteful to him?

The answer I often heard growing up, from church pulpits and discussions and children's stories and such, is that Jonah was racist, or xenophobic at least, and that, in this respect, he represented the Jewish people in general. The *Encyclopedia Britannica* summarizes the situation like this: "the prophet Jonah, like the Jews of the day, abhors even the idea of salvation for the Gentiles."[2] This is quite an accusation. The introduction to the Book of Jonah in the *NIV Study Bible* puts it similarly:

> Nineveh, the great menace to Israel, is representative of the Gentiles. Correspondingly, stubbornly reluctant Jonah represents Israel's jealousy of her favored relationship with God and her unwillingness to share the Lord's compassion with the nations.[3]

The word "Gentile," meaning "anybody who is not Jewish," does not occur in the book of Jonah even once, nor does any comparable word. But even so, it has become a sort of popular theological position to talk as though Jonah simply didn't want to go and speak to people who weren't Jewish, nor share anything with them that he might deem good from his religious heritage.[4] Jonah, it is

2. Goetz, *Micropaedia, Vol 6*, 604.

3. Barker, *The NIV Study Bible*, 1342.

4. While the reason for Jonah's flight as discussed above seems to prevail on the popular level, several further ideas tend to recur in commentaries, and they seem to me equally odd. The most common is the theologically contrived idea that if the Assyrians repented then this would somehow equate to the fall of Jonah's own people. This idea arises out of various Biblical threads. Perhaps Jonah was afraid of the words of Moses' ominous old song, where God says: "They have provoked me to anger with their idols. So I will make them jealous with those who are no people; I will provoke them to anger with a foolish nation" (Deuteronomy 32:21). And Jesus centuries later says "The men of Nineveh will rise up at the judgment with this generation and condemn it, for they repented" (Matthew 12:41). To this tune Jerome's commentary says "the prophet knows, by the suggestion of the Holy Spirit, that the repentance of the Gentiles is the ruination of the Jews" (Hegedus, *Jerome's commentary*,

often supposed, got on the boat going the other way because he didn't like foreign people, and neither did any of his kind.

All this rhetoric about Jonah's generic Jewish racism sounds to me like generic racism against Jewish people. It is of course all too easy to look back on moral tales of times past with a sort of conceit: how foolish the protagonists were to make mistakes we would never have made! How fortunate that we are now so much wiser than they were! And of course the syndrome is only exacerbated with regard to religious texts, where to be on the wrong side of the moral of the story is to find oneself on the wrong side of its fish-wielding Deity—until, with marvelous irony, we must one day face our own conceit in the belly of some monster or other.

------

6). Calvin's commentary suggests that the ruination of the Jews was what God really wanted all along: "It might have been then, that he was sent to Nineveh, that the Lord, being wearied of the obstinacy of his own people, might afford an example of pious docility on the part of a heathen and uncircumcised nation, in order to render the Israelites more inexcusable" (Calvin, *Commentaries*, 20). Why is it so unthinkable that God would genuinely have compassion on a people simply for the sake of having compassion on them? Why are we to think that any time it appears that way, it's just God's back-handed way of spiting the Jews? –as though the whole of history were a mere contrivance to spite the Jews! Apart from being rather anti-Semitic, this racist theological tick leaves us in a catch twenty-two where, on the one hand, God's people are called to bless the nations, but on the other hand they can expect to be somehow chastised and shamed every time they do so.

Another recurring idea is that Jonah was worried about his reputation: Theodoret's commentary explains "Since he knew for certain about the streams of mercy which the One who ordered him to preach uses to govern everything, and since he was sure that if the Ninevites repented they would obtain divine mercy completely, he believed it would be unseemly for the prediction to be shown false, and that he be called a liar instead of a prophet" (Heisler, *Gnat or Apostolic Bee*, 48) That is to say, he was worried that he'd look like a false prophet for having said "forty days and Nineveh will be destroyed" (Jonah 3:4), because forty days later, there Nineveh still was. But it would seem an odd world where prophets were to be stoned every time peoples repented; and in any case, running off to sea might have raised more eyebrows amongst those who liked to talk. Really, the commission was one of such mortal horror that I think all this biblical sophistry would be the furthest thing from any prophet's mind.

Hugh Martin's commentary gives the most sensible answer to the puzzle that I can find: "Judge not, that ye be not judged" (Martin, *Jonah*, 49).

The curiosity is not so much the lack of sympathy for Jonah, but the presumptuous reasoning for why he ran. The idea of Jonah as the embodiment or microcosm of the Jewish people's alleged racism is quite beyond the remit the story itself which makes no generic statements about the Gentiles (or the Jewish people) at all. Are we supposed to imagine that, having heard God's call, the prophet sat down and thought to himself, "I cannot stand Gentiles! What shall I do?"—and then realized he might well escape this malady by hopping on a boat full of Gentiles to a far away land where he would live among Gentiles till the day he died and most likely never see another Jewish man or woman again? " . . . And he found a ship going to Tarshish: so he paid the fare thereof."

In fact the book positively exudes the warmth of the relationship between Jonah and his (gentile) mariners. He clearly hadn't spent the voyage cooped up by himself in a silently introspective gloom, as the sermon at the beginning of *Moby Dick* would have it.[5] In the shockingly outspoken manner that he keeps throughout the book he converses freely with the sailors, as his homeland shrinks away forever behind him. He openly unburdens his heart to them, telling them even about his flight from his God, over rum and backgammon, and sea shanties, and exchanges of nautical tales. And when the storm hits and the lots are drawn he is willing to die for the crew; while the crew, on the other hand, are quite unwilling to give him up. I am always struck by just how long this tense scene of separation goes on for.[6]

So where does such an irrationally racist reading of the tale come from? Perhaps it is that tendency towards religious parricide

5. "With slouched hat and guilty eye, skulking from his God; prowling among the shipping like a vile burglar. [. . .] 'Point out my state-room, Sir,' says Jonah now, 'I'm travel-weary; I need sleep.' 'Thou lookest like it,' says the Captain, 'there's thy room.' Jonah enters, and would lock the door, but the lock contains no key. Hearing him foolishly fumbling there, the Captain laughs lowly to himself, and mutters something about the doors of convicts' cells being never allowed to be locked within." (Melville, *Moby Dick*, 43-45)

6. The rabbinic text *Pirke de Rabbi Eliezer* has it that the beloved mariners, having witnessed Jonah's miraculous salvation, then land back at Joppa and go to the temple in Jerusalem where each are circumcised and make vows to Jonah's God. See Limburg, *Jonah*, 107.

that E. P. Sanders noted, that one religion feels compelled to de-throne its predecessor by painting an unsavory picture of it.[7] Per-haps it's contrived as evidence for that alarmingly common (and racist) misconception that Jesus was compelled to start Christian-ity because Judaism was racist. Perhaps it's part of that retrospec-tive mangling of a story through the wheels of different eras of history: the Book of Jonah, like all others, is read by Christians in the light of whichever era they feel a theological or traditional attachment to, and no doubt the anti-Semitism of Martin Luther and of the Nicene Council are both still with us, to our shame and impoverishment.[8] We cannot help reading old texts through the

7. "The Position is basically this: *We* (the Christians, or the true Chris-tians) believe in grace and forgiveness. Those religious qualities *characterize* Christianity, and thus could not have been present in the religion from which Christianity came. Otherwise, why the split? But the Jews, or at least their lead-ers, the Pharisees, did not believe in repentance and forgiveness. They not only would not extend forgiveness to their own errant sheep, they would kill anyone who proposed to do so.

The position is so incredible that I wish it were necessary only to state it in order to demonstrate its ridiculousness." (Sanders, *Jesus and Judaism*, 202)

8. To quote from Martin Luther's tract *The Jews and Their Lies:* "Be on your guard against the Jews, knowing that wherever they have their synagogues, nothing is found but a den of devils in which sheer selfglory, conceit, lies, blas-phemy and defaming of God and men are practiced." And while we hold the Nicene Council in some reverence for its consolidation of the Christian canon and creeds, they also decided to distinguish Easter from the Jewish Passover festival, which had up until then been celebrated by many Churches as one and the same festival. The decision itself is perhaps innocuous enough, but Constantine's written order to the Churches on the matter is most telling of the anti-Semitic rationale behind it:

"It was, in the first place, declared improper to follow the custom of the Jews in the celebration of this holy festival, because, their hands having been stained with crime, the minds of these wretched men are necessarily blinded. By rejecting their custom, we establish and hand down to succeeding ages one which is more reasonable, and which has been observed ever since the day of our Lord's sufferings. Let us, then, have nothing in common with the Jews, who are our adversaries . . . how can they entertain right views on any point who, after having compassed the death of the Lord, being out of their minds, are guided not by sound reason, but by an unrestrained passion, wherever their innate madness carries them . . . Therefore this irregularity must be corrected, in order that we may no more have any thing in common with those parricides and the murderers of our Lord" (Theodoret, *Ecclesiastical History*, 32).

concerns of the present and I am openly doing exactly this, but it is something else to interpret stories neither through the present nor through the era that they belong to, but rather through the concerns of some other era which we have uncritically idealized such that the rest of history must be shoved through the grinder of its limited interests.

The other side of the problem is the very strange habit among the writers of the Hebrew Bible of painting themselves in a rather dubious light. While most people will go to great pains to be shown in the most complimentary light for posterity, these people were determined to roll around in the muck and write all the sordid details of their failings across their faces before any record of themselves be kept. Pascal marks this oddity well, although not many other people seem to have noticed:

> Lovingly and faithfully they hand on this book in which Moses declares that they have been ungrateful towards God throughout their lives, that he knows they will be still more so after his death, but that he calls heaven and earth to witness against them that he told them often enough. He declares that God will in the end grow angry with them and disperse them among the peoples of the earth, that as they angered him by worshipping gods who were not their gods, so he will provoke them by calling on a people who are not his people, and he wishes all his words to be preserved eternally and his book to be placed in the ark of the covenant to serve forever as a witness against them.[9]

Obviously they had not understood the conventionally accepted purpose of keeping one's stories and legends. The recording of histories has tended to be a means of self preservation where the power and the privilege of ruling classes is justified by records of pure genealogies that go all the way back to the gods, of just wars fairly and squarely won, and of the greatness and wisdom of one ruler to the next. All this pomp about the past is contrived to strengthen a civilization's place in the future and grasp at the

---

9. Pascal, *Pensées*, 144.

immortality that civilizations naturally desire. Jonah on the other hand continues in the bizarre tradition of Moses and his friends by giving us yet another story full of his own problems and conflicts, a story which is more interested in asserting the importance of civilizations other than his own. The irony of it all is that the one people whose histories consistently predict and record their own failure and demise seem to have outlasted most of the others.

Given this unusual approach to recording their stories I think it would be ungracious to read them as we might read others. There is a remarkable meanness and stupidity in the constant sermonizing against the failures of Biblical Israel that goes on in some Christian circles. It is the negative imprint of blowing your own trumpet: stamping on someone else's because they refused to blow it for themselves. Who is the Pharisee and who is the tax collector here?[10] We once again witness the inability of pride to comprehend the wisdom of humiliation.

I would like, then, to argue precisely the opposite to that which is too often said about the Book of Jonah. This tale is not an example of generic Jewish racism. On the contrary, Jewish religious tradition here presents us with an ideal so universal, so pluralistic and so generous that most reasonable persons would say it surely goes much too far.

To make our argument we will return to the original question: why *did* Jonah get on the boat? Why is he the only prophet in the Bible who runs from his calling? For all the ingenious suggestions that have been made and asserted over two millennia or so, a brief sketch of the people of Nineveh will suggest a very obvious possibility. The Assyrians, who ruled from Nineveh, were the Nazis of the ancient world. They were, and still are, legendary for their fetishized brutality which expressed itself in the very worst that a darkened imagination could think of. They constructed lavish towers out of the severed heads of their enemies. They would make spectacles of screaming terror by publicly skinning people alive. They would leave people impaled through orifices by lubricated

10. We refer here to Jesus' parable about the difference between pride and humility in Luke 18:9–14.

stakes pushed in far enough to upset the internal organs without causing an overly hurried death. They would bury people up to their necks and allow their bodies to decompose in their own filth while they still lived. And it was the King's royal privilege to decide what imaginative horrors the vanquished would be subjected to after a battle was won. The Assyrians were on Israel's doorstep and the fear of falling into their hands was a very real one. In the end it is exactly what happened.

Can you imagine a Jewish man stood on a soapbox at the Nuremburg rallies and loudly shouting that the Nazi project would come to nothing good, and that they should all repent in dust and ashes? I should think not. No one with anything left in their head would do it. While the Book of Jonah may well go deeper in its exploration of the prophet's complicated feelings toward the power of Nineveh, the terrifying absurdity of the idea is reason enough to get on a boat going the other way without anyone needing to accuse anyone of being racist. And while no sensible person would be willing to embrace the idea that one people are worthy of love and compassion and another are not, many of the same people would be just as unsettled to have to contemplate love and compassion for sadistic, murderous Nazis. The suggestion itself feels unjust and distasteful.

The problem, I think, is the mistake of noticing the content of the book without noticing the bizarre, inexplicable and miraculous existence of the book itself, as Pascal does. Why did they write these stories down? Having only the content of the tale to go on (and probably no clue who the Ninevites were), plenty of people feel quite ready to berate the troubled prophet for his lack of piety and obedience. But when we ponder the *existence* of the book, and how it came to be: the fact that some Jewish scribe decided to write down this story of God's compassion for a people who had (by the time of composition) long since conquered Israel and subjected them to all its routine horrors and atrocities, is remarkable. The fact that the book was not then rejected, banned and burned by more moderate and sensible people for its distasteful sympathy toward the diabolically evil seems to me inexplicable. The fact that the book was then selected to be canonized as holy writ in the Jewish Bible is, finally, miraculous. And yet there is little sympathy for Jonah these days.

So, it is in this respect that I say that, far from being an example of ancient Jewish racism, the book of Jonah is a pillar of scandalously progressive values and of a universal human vision. This vision seems to me to be threaded through the whole Hebrew Bible, which, from one end to the other, finds its telos in the affirmation and blessing of all the peoples of the world. But of all of them, no book of the Hebrew canon says this more provocatively and shockingly than Jonah, and nothing is more shocking than the presence of Jonah in the canon. If there is racism and jealousy involved I'm sure it can be found at the end of the anti-Semitic rhetoric that has dogged various turns of Western history. I am prayerfully hopeful that we are moving toward a new time of readiness to learn from the great Hebrew tradition of confessing one's *own* stubbornness, jealousy and pride, rather than berating others for confessing theirs.

3

The City of Fishes

Jonah in children's books ~ On our disinterest in chapters three and four ~ On the real monster of the book ~ On the long walk to hell ~ On Jonah's two fears ~ The Book of Jonah as a political tract ~ On radical enemy-love and radical non-violence ~ On rebirth as a political theme ~ Jonah's previous job

THE BOOK OF JONAH makes a very good children's story. Stories for the very young often benefit from two things: a comprehensible moral point and an animal character or two. Even the terrifying watery apocalypse of Noah and his ark becomes a digestible story for children with all the animals thrown in. But it's true to say that for a great many of the children's books retelling the story of Jonah's bane, the tale is more or less over by the time Jonah is spat back up on the beach at the end of chapter two. That first half of the book makes a very coherent tale, with a beginning, a middle and an end: a task is set, there is a crisis of obedience, the crisis is resolved and Jonah finally agrees to do what he is told. And this is a moral that generations of parents have found very agreeable.

In this sense, the story makes for a very potent and rather individualistic fable about a person, and this person's relationship to God and duty. It says something like: *a life of obedience is more straightforward* or *if you don't do what God says he will send a whale to eat you up*—a parable of cause and effect: *keep to your responsibilities or you'll end up in trouble.* To go into too much detail about the second half of the book only confuses the whole matter, with gourds and worms and threats of suicide, and with Jonah lapsing back into gloom and resentment about his task after all.

Perhaps it's because so many of us know Jonah only from children's stories (or from other people who only know Jonah from children's stories) that the tale remains an individualistic moral fable to some. Or perhaps the image of the whale, which will only grow in its profundity as we grow older, remains the most engaging element of the tale and we never quite get past it. Or perhaps it is related to our quasi-Marcionite practice of allegorizing the strange and unwieldy material of the Hebrew Bible, and transforming it into more user-friendly material for the religion of inner spirituality and of behaving oneself that became predominant as the Jewish sect called Christianity was steadily absorbed into the politics and Platonisms of the Hellenistic world.[1]

Jonah as a moral tale about obedience is a start, but I'm sure this is not what the book is really about, and neither is the whale the biggest beast that swims darkly through it. The beast that the book cowers before, rages against, thoughtfully circles, miserably embraces and finally despairs over is *empire*—the Neo-Assyrian Empire. We have discussed above the unique pleasure they took in devising horrible ways to publicly mutilate people, but they were

1. Marcion was a heretic—it was decided—from the second century. He asserted that the God of Jesus Christ and the New Testament couldn't possibly be the same as the volatile and uncouth deity of the Hebrew Bible who created this world of base and dysfunctional matter. And so, while the New Testament was to be recognized as holy writ, Marcion said that the Hebrew Bible was to be rejected. In the end it was Marcion who was rejected and the Hebrew Bible was kept and recognized as being of the same God as the New Testament. However, since Platonic ideas about the nastiness of matter prevailed in the Roman world, and since Jewish people were at that time thought of in more or less the way we think of Jihadists today, the narratives of the Hebrew Bible were rinsed of their historical, social and political message and reduced to a series of allegories about a personal and inward spirituality. So while Marcion was expelled, his point was nevertheless partly taken on board.

also quite exceptional in their time for a number of other reasons. They were the first empire to attempt globalization, the first to embark on the concerted project of making the known world *Assyria*. They were the first to make Assyrian citizens of peoples who were not Assyrian and who lived in the faraway lands they had conquered. They were the first to try to impose one language upon the many peoples across their conquered dominion, so that native languages were lost and the Aramaic tongue of the Assyrians prevailed; so that six hundred years after the fall of the Assyrian empire we find that Jesus is still speaking the language of that empire. They were the first to form a standing army, made up of men who were not conscripted Assyrians, or mercenaries or conquered people who had no choice (although they also used all of the above as war fodder), but men whose full time job was to be the Assyrian army, and they did indeed become an irresistible force. The Neo-Assyrian Empire as it existed in the days of Jonah was, by some people's reckoning, the first proper empire in history. Their fetish for violence and their imperial spirit expressed itself in their way of decimating not only peoples, but also *peoplehood*, by deporting the surviving peoples of conquered lands and scattering them across the empire until the various languages, religions, stories and cultures of vanquished peoples were gradually dissipated and lost in the imperial mush; until the world was Assyria. And of course variations of this model have prevailed ever since; never more so than today.

Nineveh, perched on the river Tigris and known as the City of Fishes,[2] was the seat of the Assyrian empire and "the King of Nineveh" was the lord, or the tyrant, of the known world. His diabolical squirming brain and the pomp of "that great city" were the epicenter of new kind of human plague—a parasite clamped onto the edge of the world sucking it dry and making a spreading circular blotch of desolation around itself almost as far as anyone could

2. The ancient cuneiform script represented the "Nine" part of Nineveh with a pictograph of a fish in a house. Perhaps the suggestion is that the terror of the great fish in which the prophet was housed was the story's mirror image of the terrible city which houses the fish. The Hebrew prophets loved to play with words.

see. The prophet Nahum speaks for many when he protests: "Woe to the bloody city, all full of lies and plunder—no end to the prey [. . .] upon whom has not come your unceasing evil?"[3]

Now, it is one thing to rail against the seat of oppression from the periphery. In fact, it can make a person quite popular. To Jonah, on the other hand, God gives a different task: "Arise, go to Nineveh, that great city, and cry against it; for their wickedness is come up before me."[4]

It is no wonder that Jonah boards a boat to Tarshish, which by some people's reckoning was in Spain—as far as you could possibly get from the viral horror emanating from Nineveh. I expect if he had any notion that there was anything across the Atlantic besides the end of the world he would have got into another boat and kept going even if he had to paddle all the way himself.

The Hebrew word for "wickedness" ("their wickedness is come up before me," says God) is not to do with moral failure or something like that (as we might denote with the word for "sin," meaning to fail, or fall, or miss). Rather it speaks of malice, violence and deadliness. Jonah was not a protestant missionary imploring people towards religious conversion. He was a Hebrew prophet confronting the politics of empire and the diabolical greed of imperial violence with the entirely different and bizarre politics of the Kingdom of God, which he himself spends the rest of the story struggling to make any good sense of.

From hearing the story as a child, I had always imagined that the city of Nineveh was on the coast, and that when Jonah's slobbered and half-digested frame flopped out of the fish's mouth onto the sand, that he picked himself up, walked up the beach and through the gates of "that wicked city." I expect it's because it takes a chapter to get out to sea and a chapter for the whale to bring him back, but then the next chapter just picks up the story as he enters the city. In fact, Nineveh is (or was) in northern Iraq. It was about four hundred miles from the coast, as I judge it by looking at a map and measuring with my finger. There was no chance of

3. Nahum 3:1 & 19.
4. Jonah 1:2.

jumping enthusiastically from one jaw-dropping miracle to the next. Rather, there was a very long walk to hell, during which every terrifying possibility might present itself to the desperate man's mind. As he lay there vomited up on the beach, did he feel saved, as he had done in the belly of the whale? Or did he feel doomed?

We then read of his lonely entry into the City of Blood; the epicenter of darkness, a place filled with the stories and images of beheadings, impalings and skinnings, where nothing was familiar and every thing and every sound and every person was strange, malicious and other. And he spends a day walking around in, I suppose, terrified anticipation of the moment when he will have to open his mouth and speak with his foreign tongue against this irresistible force of triumphalistic terror. There is no promise given in the story that he would not end up being burned or mangled or buried alive, and I should think it would be difficult to imagine any other outcome. And then after taking in his last miserable day of life, he says this: "Yet forty days and Nineveh shall be overthrown!"[5] And then he waits to have his throat cut.

———————————

There is a strange thing that sometimes occurs in dreams or visions or stories, where a situation transforms completely and yet holds on to some kind of continuity, so much so that one almost fails to notice the paradigm shift. You are at a dinner party with friends and you leave the room only to re-enter and find that you are in a room full of animals; and you carry on. A man is forever stranded on an island and longs only to get home: next we see him, in his city apartment, overdosing. Two young men escape from a city where their revolutionary leader has just been executed, but when they sit down to eat with a vagrant who's joined them a few hours before they suddenly see that the vagrant *is* their revolutionary leader.[6] As the world becomes more strange, unpredictable

5. Jonah 3:4.

6. The first is a dream I'd guess lots of people have had in some form or other. The second example is taken from a sequence in the TV series *Lost*. Film (or television) seems to be more inclined to experiment with this kind of paradigm shifting narrative device, perhaps because films are made of a succession

and uncertain, the protagonists and their problems become ever clearer. We might call it an apocalyptic paradigm shift: a moment when everything switches over to an impossible alternative reality, only to find that this surreal new situation reveals deeper truths about everything that has gone on before.

When the King of Nineveh hears about Jonah's kamikaze sermonette and, unimaginably, decides to call the whole city to repent of its violent imperial project, when the City of Blood and of goose-stepping triumphal evil turns in a moment into a hu-miliated penitent doused in sackcloth and ashes, when the known world seems for a moment to have been saved from that cyclone of brutal tyranny by the eight words of a Jewish vagrant, it becomes apparent that there is something our protagonist fears more than the horrible violence of empire: this being the compassionate poli-tics of the Kingdom of God. I expect we are no different. It is the moment when we realize that we do not want Nineveh to repent. We do not want pedophiles to be reformed. We do not want the casino bankers to return to their jobs as better men. We do not want News International to become a decent establishment. We don't want Nazis to grow old. One cannot, without a bit of self-de-ception, avoid the feeling that the God of the Bible is at times un-realistic about what sort of situation can reasonably be redeemed. We want a world without such people, and we don't feel safe in a world where such evil might be redeemed lest the redeemed lapse back into their evil. If the wrath of God is slow in coming, then the world must be a world of walls and boundaries and prisons, locking down society's nightmares until they're spent.

The prophet, who has more emotional intelligence and hon-esty than most of us, comes suddenly into focus as the world turns to water all about him. The problem is revealed:

> "Was this not my saying when I was yet in my country?
> Therefore I fled before unto Tarshish: for I knew that

---

of edits, whereas prose is the continuous flow of words. The film *Upstream Color* is an interesting example of a story made up of a more-or-less continu-ous succession of these jarring shifts. The last example is from Luke 24:13–35.

thou art a gracious God, and merciful, slow to anger, and
of great kindness, and repentest thee of the evil."[7]

The grace of God is awful to us because the proper response
to evil is to fear it and desire its destruction, not to love it and
desire its redemption. We can all think of concrete examples that
will make our skin crawl. What God says to Jonah in the end reveals what Jonah had guessed about God at the story's beginning:
that God so loved the empire: "Should I not," says the Deity, "spare
Nineveh, that great city, wherein are more than sixscore thousand
persons that cannot discern between their right hand and their left
hand; and also much cattle?"[8]

While the book of Jonah makes a brilliant children's story, it
is not a children's story, nor is it a story about a whale, but about
an empire. It is a tract about radical enemy-love and radical non-
violence. The word radical is not used lightly, since in all history
no enemy has ever seemed less human or more evil than the Neo-
Assyrian Empire. The call to have loving compassion for such
monsters would be distasteful to the extreme, and I repeat, it is
miraculous that the book survived at all let alone was canonized
as holy writ by anyone. The call to respond to such an empire, not
with swords and shields and armed resistance, but by going and
talking things over with them, is absurd. If anyone but God had
proposed the idea, Jonah would have laughed and said, "you have
no idea what you're talking about." This is, as we mentioned earlier,
a terrible call.

The revelation of our apocalyptic paradigm shift occasioned by
the unprecedented repentance of those imperialist beasts might
perhaps take us back to our original theme of the prophet's humiliation: his three days in the dark and cavernous belly of the
whale, where there is nothing beyond the walls but an oblivion

---

7. To the rather abstract debate about whether we might compel God
towards a change of mind, we might now, with Jonah, add the question of
whether we can prevent God from changing it.

8. Jonah 4:11.

of cold water and where the ceiling drip, drip, drips. I think we left off with the following questions: from what was he there being transformed? And to what end?

The only other reference to "Jonah son of Amittai" in the Hebrew bible is found in the histories recorded in 2 Kings, and it gives us a passing image of his previous life in Israel's political world. Here we read that King Jereboam the son of Joash "restored the boarder of Israel from Lebo-hamath as far as the Sea of Arabah, according to the word of the Lord, the God of Israel, which he spoke by his servant Jonah the son of Amittai."[9] It seems that Jonah was instrumental in expanding and keeping Israel's borders with the Arameans to the north, who were all that stood between Israel and the Assyrian war machine: "for the Lord saw the affliction of Israel was very bitter: for there was none left, bond or free, and there was none to help Israel."[10] Perhaps now the meaning of the great humiliation and rebirth emerges. Jonah was the prophet who established the boundaries that kept the barbaric enemy out. His business was that line in the ground between the self and the dangerous other. But then he became the prophet who disregarded them. In the time when everyone was burning bridges, Jonah found himself building one to hell. What shook his soul there in the gloom, that all the structures that had brought safety, security and certainty were collapsed to reveal a glimpse of the uncontainable and dangerous God beyond them? How does a person go from wanting to keep his life to being ready to give it away? He was called to move on from the boundary logic of "an eye for an eye" towards the absurd logic of turning the other cheek, or offering one's neck. He was called to turn his allegiance from the boundary that had given a sense of safety and certainty to the God who is God over all boundaries. He was to turn his attention from the boundary that had kept the enemy out, to the image of God in the enemy on the other side of it. Through the hell of the whale's

9. 2Kings 14: 25.
10. 2Kings 14:26.

belly he had to be reborn, because politics of this kind will require rebirth.[11]

What then do we learn of the meaning of baptism as Jonah undergoes it in the belly of the whale? The whale was not sent to return him to reason, but to unhinge him from it. The whale was not sent to return him to his senses but to free him from them, and to open his vision to the possibility of acts of apparent madness. Baptism is a political act in which we become free from our obligation to the politics of the old order with its borders, boundaries and its imperatives of competition, expansion, security, survival and conquest. To use Waetjen's language, when Jonah was reborn from the mouth of the whale he became "wholly unobliged."[12] But this is not merely a declaration or a statement, but an openness to a totally transformative process; to a death and a rebirth. An openness to being utterly dislodged by God from the politics of the current order, and called, in some way, to the task of interrupting and redeeming it into the Kingdom of God.

"No one can enter the Kingdom without first being reborn", says Jesus, "and the one who wants to keep his own life will lose it, but the one who gives it up for the sake of the Kingdom receives it back again." And then he marched into the hands of the Romans under the title of Messiah—meaning political liberator—but he took no weapons and he had no army. Some have mistakenly thought that it was because he didn't think his mission was political; but they only think this way because they can't imagine a politics without war.[13] His mission was as political as Jonah's was, and it is Jonah he points to to explain himself. It was through the politics of radical enemy-love that the yeast of the Kingdom began to overturn the empire.

11. "In order to love your enemies, you must begin by analysing self." – Martin Luther King Jr. From the Sermon *Love Your Enemies*, given November 17th 1957.

12. Myers, *Binding the Strong Man*, 129.

13. It has been said that politics is merely the continuation of perpetual war. See Foucault, *Society Must Be Defended*, 15.

4

The Two Horses

On the peculiar absence of chapter five ~ On Jonah's argument with the Deity ~ On the final paradox: the call is too terrible and yet it stands ~ On various enemies ~ On the greatness of deeds and the futility of opinions ~ On grass roots solidarity and on speaking truth to empire ~ On Jonah's trauma, and the building of bridges to hell

I MAKE NO EXAGGERATION by saying that the story we consider here is the most progressive story I can think of ever having read. It is bizarre and unexpected to be saying this sort of thing about a text from the ancient world, when, as we know, all humanity were dull and backward. This text makes the leftists of the current era seem positively conservative. While the radicals of the present age rightly call the powerful to act at least justly towards the power-less, the Book of Jonah calls upon the powerless, and asks them for nothing less than proactive compassion for the utterly tyrannical despots of empire. The book seems to have a counterintuitive idea of where history's real power lies, and where its real wretchedness is. And all this from a religious text! It is no wonder that even the book's protagonist, from start to finish, cannot accept the kind of politics being suggested here.

And so we arrive at one of the book's literary peculiarities. It is quite bad storytelling to go from beginning to middle to end without the main character developing in some way, but Jonah's final exchanges with God in chapter four relay the depressing sentiment that he feels no different about the whole appalling business than he did at the start of chapter one. I wonder if perhaps we are missing a chapter? God's closing declaration of compassion on those who seem irredeemably terrible give us a stark theological source for radical non-violent enemy-love as well as for equality and universal human rights; but what are we to make of the pregnant silence that comes after? How does Jonah respond? What does he say? What does he do next? Does he make his peace with this alarming new situation and live the rest of his days in Nineveh as an unlikely national treasure? Were his bones really entombed in that ill-fated mosque in Mosul, which is indeed the place where Nineveh itself used to sit?[1] Or did he return to Israel and live in abject poverty with his widowed mother as some rabbinic stories tell, perhaps unable to stomach his old job as the border patrol?[2] Was he changed by his strange story, or was he unchanged? Was he made by it, or unmade? Did he actually survive his rebirth, or did he manage to accomplish the task but was himself miscarried

---

1. The shrine of Jonah was originally housed in a church which later became the mosque of the Prophet Yunus (Jonah). The ubiquitous prophet is highly esteemed in Islam, being the only one of the twelve "minor" prophets of the Hebrew Bible to be referenced in the Qur'an. His story is recounted in Sura 37:139–148.

2. A first century text called *The Lives of the Prophets* has it that Jonah's mother was none other than the widow of Zarephath (1 Kings 17) who hosts the fugitive prophet Elijah, and the three of them live through the drought together on a handful of flour and little bit of oil that never runs out. And indeed it is Jonah, the widow's son, who then dies of some illness and is raised again by Elijah who then goes off to confront King Ahab and the prophets of Baal. Perhaps it was to this that Jonah returns in the missing chapter five? This rather bleak image of the marginal survival of the faithful poor has a number of implications, one being that, in this apocryphal Jewish text, Jonah (who, as we are told by some Christian commentators, resented the very thought of any goodwill towards the gentiles) was actually portrayed as the son of a gentile woman. See again, Limburg, *Jonah*, 102.

in the process? The story is unfinished, or at least open-ended, and we flounder confusedly into the vacant space after it.[3]

While the ending may be open, it remains the case that in what is written there is a refusal to show any sign of the prophet's acceptance of this terrible grace. He accepts the terrible *call* when he's up to his knees in bile, but the terrible grace of God on the monsters of the age—even to the heart of that blood soaked empire—is never accepted, and we are left to wonder whether or not he ever does.

Though it seems impious to say so, there is a sort of human empathy that characterizes the Hebrew Bible, in which God's call is portrayed as being on the one hand good, truthful and right, but on the other hand intolerable, awful and impossible. Moses is expected to instigate a revolution and lead a homeless people without ever losing his temper or hitting any rocks. The people of Israel are expected to be the only people making do without a king even when it drives them into social, political and moral chaos. Uriah is expected to get the covenant box from one place to another without ever touching it. King Saul is expected to do nothing but sit on his hands and wait for Samuel while there is mutiny, and Samuel is late. "You have deceived me!" says Jeremiah. "O, Lord God, Please cease!" says Amos. "Will you not hear?" asks Habakkuk.

If I were to hazard a theological statement, I might say that the God of the Hebrews is not strictly reasonable. If, in the age of

3. I recommend the exercise of writing a big "5" on a page and drawing up some imagined conclusion to the tale. Do it with some others and compare your speculations, and of course please send them to me.

One rather beautiful example can be found in its entirety in James Limburg's commentary, an Arabic retelling of the story from *the Tales of the Prophets of al-Kisa'i*, circa 1200CE. Here, Jonah leaves Nineveh, disillusioned, and finds hospitality in the home of a potter. God tells Jonah to tell the potter to destroy all his pottery, and so the potter, of course, throws him out. God says, "Thou didst tell the potter what thou didst tell him, and he put thee out of his house, yet thou wishest the destruction of a hundred thousand and more!" After a few more such lessons Jonah is finally won over to God's compassion. Then he is reunited with his wife and his son (who had been acosted by a wolf earlier), and he finds his lost wealth in the belly of a fish that they buy at the market. The three return to their hometown where they live out their days happily. See Limburg, *Jonah*, 115-18.

reason, the biblical God YHWH was described as being utterly reasonable, I expect it is because YHWH was not so much their God as reason itself was.[4] The words and the stories of the Bible exist in a frank and honest tension between God and humanity, and the tension is never more vivid than it is when God asks, "Doest thou well to be angry?" And then Jonah responds with a startling abandonment to the truth, "I do well to be angry, even unto death."[5]

It is all very well to agree, at the end of the book of Jonah, that God is right and Jonah is wrong, but it would be quite false to talk, with an air of condescending piety, as though we have really accepted what God has said. We have not. If we think we have it's probably because we've set the bar low from the start by saying that Jonah was just racist (as were all the Jews!). This way we have already learned the lesson before we've begun, or so we think, and the story has nothing new to teach us. But all those writers and commentators and preachers who have talked about Jonah as though he were just a stubborn, prejudiced and over-emotional sort of person, I would like to see them march through the gates of Mosul in Northern Iraq to beg an audience with the Islamic State militants who now occupy the city, saying, *You can cut my head off if you want it, but, either way, I've come to tell you that you should stop everything because your political project is both wrong and doomed.* I know nobody who has done anything like this. And I hear only stories of a few remarkable people who have. It is an absurd and unreasonable thing to do. The book does not invite us to an idiotic gung-ho response about how right God is and how wrong Jonah is. Rather, it invites us to move towards a call so terrible that even when the story's curtain falls the protagonist still cannot accept it.

Jonah was not called to criticize the enemy from a distance, as Nahum was. Nor was he called to muster force or resistance, as he had been in his previous job. Rather he was called *to go to the*

---

4. Alas, for Francis Schaeffer's lament over the lost circle of reason which used to encompass both God and creation. Shaeffer, *The God Who is There*, 21.

5. Jonah 4:4 & 9.

terrible 'other' in search of the image of God. If the Book of Jonah is about anything, I believe this is it.

It is a book for the idealist; calling us to the most radical political ideal imaginable. It is a book is for the realist, since even the protagonist can't stomach its ridiculous ideal. And in the end it is a book for the audacious, stubbornly upholding its impossible ideal anyway.

The call is terrible. And yet the call stands.

On the question of enemies.

The whole matter is confusing because some people think they have all kinds of enemies who aren't really enemies, while others are completely clueless about how many enemies they actually do have, or why they even have them. And then some people know all too well that they have enemies, and their enemies agree. In any case, the first step towards loving our enemies is to acknowledge them.

Life on the ground has tended to recognize two kinds of enemies arching over it on one side and the other. As John of Patmos saw it, there is the conqueror who rides from the West on a white horse, wearing a crown of legitimacy and sovereignty and bringing its imperial peace through violently righteous conquest. And on the other hand there is the barbaric warlord who rides from the East on a red horse bringing a sword of war and chaos against the conqueror's power.[6] There's the empire you live under and the counter empire that rages against it. The Romans and the Barbarians; the Crusaders and the Mohammedans; the Capitalists and the Communists: Western democracy and Sharia law.

---

6. Our allusion here is to Revelation chapter six: the vision of the four horsemen. The other two horses are the black horse of economic greed and the domination of resources, and the dappled horse of pestilence, famine and death; these two being two sides of the same coin, just as the white and the red horse are. The four make a compelling picture of the powers which plague human history and which must finally be overthrown: imperialism, war, economic injustice and endemic poverty.

To speak of the first kind, The Oppressor, we must look to our own order with its history of imperialism, its economic power, its military dominance, and its citizenry organized around a consumerist pattern of life: the neo-liberal order that is drunk on oil and falling down the stairs as I write. This is the power under which we live. We speak its language and we live in its narratives and constructs, and under its law and order.

In what sense we may recognize it as an enemy is not straightforward, because while some of us get the bad end of the stick, many of us are dangerously comfortable, and those multitudes of others who are violently destroyed by it are always far away. It may be that we recognize this empire as an enemy because we ourselves have suffered under it. Or alternatively we might take a stance against it out of solidarity with some other: the climate, the dispossessed underclass, the orphans of the last war, or the orphans of the next war. Or perhaps—and most dangerously of all—we've become conscious of a more loving vision of the world that it blocks off for the sake of its own burdensome continuation.

If we are willing, as I think today we must be, to recognize our enemy in the people who represent the power of the white horse from the West, we can't do without enemy-love. Love them we must, because we too will need the same grace. Few of us in the West can avoid embodying the dark role of this empire to some degree, because we make up the market and the demand that justify its environmental pillaging, its wars for resources, and the global racket in slave labor that keeps it alive. The Oppressor is the enemy whose hand we darkly hold, and from whose shadow we must ourselves emerge.

The other kind of enemy we will call The Foreign Terror; and we are of course talking about the Middle Eastern jihadists with their terror camps and their knives and suicide bombs, and the communists with their nuclear tests and giant pictures of their great leaders hanging everywhere, and the Russians with their scorned and vengeful iron-man presidents and their triumphal tanks and tiny cars, and even the Eastern European migrants with gold teeth and head scarves, and the tattooed Mexican fruit-pickers who, as we are often told, are pillaging the noble economies of the West to naught. The Foreign Terror is never the dominant power under whose language, myths and propaganda we live, but rather its contender—the outside threat that seeks to destroy it. It is the red horse from the East that violently shatters the peace that the white horse from the West brought about by its own violence. Whether or not this or that Foreign Terror is really an enemy of any sort at all is always muddied by the reality that our vision of the red rider from the East is largely given to us by the media powers of the empire we live in, which has its own reasons for demonizing others and maintaining a helpful degree of domestic fear.[7]

On the other hand, while the empire will make enemies out of whoever it will to excuse whichever wars it finds expedient, it would be ridiculous to talk as though all of our enemies are merely the fictions of our propagandists. One does not rule the world the way the West has without making enemies. Nor is the spirit of empire peculiar to the West. In fact, the story of Jonah and his death-march to the City of Blood leads us precisely to the place where nobody wants to go: to the ruins of his shrine in the city of Mosul in Northern Iraq, where Nineveh used to be—blown up by ISIS militants who have taken the city and spread across the region with the stated aim of establishing their own new empire, and with a violence entirely comparable with the ancient Assyrians.[8] While Western violence takes great pains to keeps itself off

7. During the writing of this essay, on 11th January 2015, Fox News has just announced that the city of Birmingham, in which I live, is apparently populated entirely by Muslims and that "Non-Muslims simply don't go there," and also that parts of London are now policed under Sharia law.

8. It took me a long time to stumble across yet another strand of this great tale which will, I expect, have been blindingly obvious to some people. The story goes roughly like this: Alas, Jonah in the end proves sadly correct in his eight word sermon, and in the mid-seventh century the Neo Assyrian Empire descends into infighting and civil war. Being thus weakened, its reign of terror is finally ended by its old Akkadian brethren, the Babylonians. Then, under the rule of one power after another—the Medes, the Persians, the Greeks, the Romans and so on—the Assyrians become an oddly resilient Diaspora living across Mesopotamian lands.

It then happens that the Assyrians, along with a number of other Semitic

of YouTube, these upload their killings directly. And in what sense are these outbreaks of violence, the forming of new powers and the vying for lands in the Middle East being addressed to us in our faraway world of humdrum consumer capitalism? How did we make such bitter enemies? What is it about the structures of my life that they have cost some distant other? It seems that everything is connected.

Whether people are more worried about the white horse or the red one generally depends, with deflating predictability, on which way they lean politically.[9] The issues are obscured by

---

peoples of Mesopotamia, are among the first peoples to embrace Christianity, between the first and third centuries. (Some traditions have it that the Assyrian Church can be traced back to 33CE, which relates, I think, to a remarkable story which involves the apostles Thomas and Thaddaeus and a Mesopotamian Prince called Abgar of Edessa who had allegedly exchanged letters with Jesus himself. See Eusebius, *History of the Church*, 65-70). From here on the Assyrians are recognized as a Christian people, forming an important strand of Eastern Christianity in Iraq, Syria, Iran and beyond. And indeed Syriac, a dialect of the Assyrian's Aramaic language, is still used today as the liturgical language of many Eastern churches.

The nineteenth and twentieth centuries became increasingly fraught for the Assyrian Diaspora, who suffered discrimination, violence, massacres and genocide from various quarters, eventually leading many Assyrians to flee for Europe and America. And now that the City of Blood has become a city of blood once again, it is none other than Jonah's Assyrians—the Christians of Mosul on the Nineveh Plains—who are now being brutalized by Islamic State militants.

Meanwhile, to consider our current state of enmity towards the Local Other, I note that my own country, the United Kingdom, has given asylum to just 216 Syrian refugees, at the last count. And in 2014 we received only eight Iraqis. While the Middle East and parts of North Africa undergo an apocalypse we recoil from the suffering, pucker up tight and hope not to be changed by it. We may mock Jonah's reticence as he goes to meet with the tyrants, but we wouldn't even take care of more than a handful of the refugees who are fleeing from them, preferring that they die in camps or drown in the Mediterranean. I'm certain that against our best efforts we will be changed by the current crisis one way or another. As long as we stay closed to their suffering we will go rotten at the core.

9. Which kind of enemy, then, is the kind that Jonah faced when he went to the Assyrians? Oppressor or Foreign Terror? Perhaps they were particularly terrifying because they were on a knife edge between the two: the foreign terror on the brink of becoming imperial oppressor by bloody conquest. The

propaganda on one side and by crude demagoguery on the other. But here we may venture to claim some clarity on two things at least: firstly, that the mystery called the Kingdom of God has no part in either kind of power. It is something entirely other and the antithesis of both;[10] and secondly, that those of us who claim allegiance to the Kingdom of God are not afforded the option of backing either horse. We are wholly unobliged to either kind of power, except for the obligation to resistance. And so, the question is not whether or not we have enemies. We do. The question is how to love them.

To pull these lofty considerations and apocalyptic visions to earth we must re-situate ourselves. If there is anything to be done, we must do it in the place where we are. And so we must look for help in the Local Other, whose otherness will be relative to our own sense of who we are and where we stand. Immigrants, refugees, ethnic minorities, pompous white middle-class progressives, outspoken conservatives, sexual minorities, old people, young people, the sorts of people who keep their dogs on a chain rather than a lead, and perhaps most significantly in the post 9/11 era, the Muslim communities. It is quite taboo, in my own circles at least, to confess any feeling of enmity towards marginal groups.[11] But the

surest test is to ask oneself whose language are we obliged to speak to get by in the world. We of the West may find any comparison with ourselves unseemly, but that is because, to many people, we *are* the Assyrians, and the structures of oppression are intrinsic to our way of life. The fact is that the West is the epicenter of empire today (although our day is getting old), and we have as much blood to answer for as the Assyrians did, though it is true to say that we are no longer the ones using severed heads as propaganda.

10. John's vision of the horsemen culminates in heaven and earth being shaken like a fig tree, and "the Kings of the earth and the great ones and the generals and the rich and the powerful, and everyone, slave and free," then say to the mountains, "fall on us and hide us from the face of him who is seated on the throne, and from the wrath of the Lamb.'" And so the fullness of the Kingdom of God finally ends the dialectic between these warring powers of history and all the poverty and pestilence they bring. See Revelation 6:15-16.

11. Though other groups are not so timid. The UK's biggest selling newspapers, The Sun and The Mail, are have become relentlessly outspoken against

enmity is revealed nevertheless in the fact that most of us don't
know anyone from this or that group of Local Others, though we
walk the same streets as them every day. Even enthusiastic and
opinionated progressives rarely have many close acquaintances
outside their own class and color. The social boundaries that
contain us are kept by some profound and purposeful power that
prevents us having a shared social experience with the other. This
silently policed segregation is the clue to the existence of a pas-
sive enmity, which is not chosen so much as accepted. The state
of nature, as it was described by Hobbes, is the war of every man
against every man.[12] The boundaries of the modern state and its
imperative of tolerance does not overcome enmity, but only manages and polices it.[13] The rhetoric of tolerance is entirely different to the politics of enemy-love. It is boundary rhetoric. It says,
*you may not like each other, but at least respect each others' space
and don't mess with each others' things.*[14] Enemy-love, on the other
hand, transgresses the boundary in order to be present with the
other, to share with the other, to hear the other, to seek the image
of God in the other, and all at the risk of self. The Local Other is
God's gift to save us all from becoming opinionated bores on all
the political abstractions elaborated above. It is difficult to know
where to start loving Rupert Murdoch or the militants of ISIS, but
all the while the Local Other awaits us, and here we must begin.

the Muslim community, immigrants, and the poor (that is, people claiming
benefits).

12. Hobbes, *Leviathan*, 88.

13. The tolerance we publicly demanded after the Charlie Hebdo shoot-
ings in Paris, between violent religious zealots and the humanists who are free
to mock them in the printing press is an entirely different thing to the love
proclaimed by the Muslims and the Jews who stood next to each other wearing
placards that said that they loved each other. One demands the maintenance
of ideological boundaries that allow us to be non-violently hateful to the other
(while the bombs fall abroad). The other shatters the boundaries with a public
proclamation of love for the other.

14. See Cavanaugh, *Theopolitical Imagination*, 15-20.

It was in this way that Jesus defined Moses' category of "neighbor" in his story of the Good Samaritan.[15] Who is my neighbor? He or she is the one that I transgress social, ethnic, political or cultural boundaries to be with. Neighborliness is not a state of mind or a disposition, but the result of a radical praxis. And so the telos of enemy-love is that the category of neighbor grows to encompass every kind of other, until, one day, the whole world fits into it.

When we hear the phrase "love your enemies"[16] its horror can be considerably reduced by internalizing the idea. We are to think kind thoughts of the people who are unkind to us and pray for those who have wronged us. This sounds like a good start, but it must be said that Jonah is not a good example of it. Rather, the prophet gives us a framework for action. He goes over to the other, into the heart of their city. Indeed, from beginning to end the prophet doesn't suffer any warm feelings towards the Assyrians, nor does he utter for them any prayer. He just goes there. Most of us exercise precisely the opposite. We may be very proud of our open-minded opinions about the other, but opinions are, in the end, just things we talk about among our own kind, and a nothingness that blows away in the wind. It is practice that matters. Only in the act, the proactive journey over the boundary to be present with the terrible other, does anything really amount to anything. Deeds not words. Enemy-love as an idea is a clanging gong. It is only something when it is done. To think kind thoughts about some enemy and carry on as before is simply to keep the tepid boundaries of tolerance and its silent enmity intact. It has nothing to do with Jonah going to the Assyrian city, and nothing to do with Jesus hung on a Roman cross. Ched Myers once put it this way:

> After all the heavy breathing we do about God, it's quite simply where one places one's body that really counts. In other words, what part of town you live in, who you hang out with, who you work alongside. And above all

---

15. Luke 10:25-37.
16. Matthew 5:44.

how many social boundaries you cross in order to be with Jesus.[17]

So when we speak of going to the other in search of the image of God, we mean *actually going there*. As Myers goes on to say: *"hope is where your ass is."* And I really believe it's true that crossing over and being with the other is a radically hopeful act that makes entirely new things possible.

Enemy-love between one group and its domestic other has a curious relation to the situation between the people and the power of empire. When we seek peace with some local other we remake society under a different sort of vision to the one that currently rules the empire. In the usual way of things our connection to each other is managed by the power at the centre of society. If someone needs help we're expected to be angry at the government for not helping them. If there is friction between communities the government needs to introduce school programs to make us all more tolerant.[18] But when we go directly to the other, when the blessing and peace of the other is *our* business rather than just the government's, then the power to shape society and to re-imagine ordinary life is taken from the centre to the edges, from the powers to the ordinary people. To put it differently; rather than appeal to the powers to do something about some other group in society, why not engage with the other to do something together about the powers? Grass roots enemy-love decentralizes power. It develops solidarity among the people, which cultivates resilience and resistance to the oppressive interests of the powers at the centre of empire. It also circumvents the crushing Western alienation that has driven hundreds of young men and women to fly out to warzones to take part in extremist bloodbaths. Grass roots enemy-love

17. Quoted from an address given at Greenbelt Festival, *Hope is Where Your Arse Is* (2007).

18. And so Cavanaugh describes the state as "a monstrosity of many separate limbs proceeding directly out of a gigantic head." He goes on, "the best the state can hope to do is to keep these individuals from interfering with each other's rights. While this can serve to mitigate the conflictual effects of individualism, it cannot hope to enact a truly social process." See again Cavanaugh, *Theopolitical Imagination*, 44.

enables us as ordinary people to become political agents shaping the world. The invisible boundaries of non-relational tolerance on the other hand keep us divided and segregated as predictable consumer units in a capitalist economy till the day we die. And so, it is through grass roots enemy-love that we reshape ordinary life. Through grass roots enemy-love we create a new political space. Through grass roots enemy-love we resist and reject the domination of the empire of the white horse, and of the red, just as we begin to collapse the dark relationship between the black horse of inequality and the dappled horse of death.

From here we may dare to love The Oppressor (to whom we are still bound) and call him to repent,[19] as Jonah did.[20] And from here we might at least stare down the path after the suffering prophet as he makes his way towards that most terrible other, The Foreign Terror, in search of the image of God.

Saint Jerome, in translating the meaning of the prophet's name offers several possibilities, but the one he finds most fitting is *Sufferer*. And very fitting it is. The other possibility, which is far more widely accepted, is *Dove*.[21] I was most stuck by what an ill fit it seemed. I can well imagine why parents wishing to call their babies Jonah would gravitate towards the latter meaning, but when we think of Jonah himself, we think of the darkness and the bile of the great fish's innards, we think of the cold storm raging under the black howling night, we think of the prophet lying under the with-

19. *Metanoia*—to change one's mind, or way, or direction. In the age of climate change, nuclear armament and the economic chaos of global capitalism, we desperately need to recover this rather taboo word.

20. Jonah didn't throw eggs, or pies, or dust and ashes at the despicable Assyrian tyrant; rather the tyrant was moved by the prophet's courageous presence to throw dust and ashes over himself. Perhaps the powerful might be more significantly changed by an encounter with people who saw their humanity than by another encounter with another person who saw them as they see themselves—as another well oiled wheel in the machine of power. Political activism is as full of hateful anger as power is full of corruption. Enemy-love exorcises our politics and our radical deeds of hate.

21. Hegedus, *Jerome's commentary*, 5.

ered and twisted gourd, we think of his knotted face hardening in the heat of the baking sun, and we think of him shouting down the streets of Nineveh, and then up at the heavens, and of his final silence; his refusal to speak the last word. Many images come to mind, but never the serene picture of a dove, or anything like it. And many themes grow in our thoughts but not the dove's theme of peace. He seems to be a troubled man from start to finish, who is ever far from peace.

But on further reflection it strikes me that peace is exactly what the story is about and peace is exactly what Jonah goes to make possible. What else do the blessed peace makers do but go to the terrible other in an unlikely search for the image of God, denouncing the empire's violence not from the safety of its edges, but in vulnerability from its epicenter? Jonah is a peace maker. The result did not gratify him, and one way or another, grace and peace will always cost the men and the women who bring them. But so the story tells, that by this sufferer, this Jewish man, who walked over the border into the place of his enemies, to speak face to face with them, peace came.

May the whale deliver us all to the terrible other, in love.

5

The Interruption

The mad prophet through Assyrian eyes ~ The Jonaic Interruption ~ On collapsing the dialectic ~ On the Interruption to end all Interruptions ~ On the prayer of forgiveness and the trauma resolved ~ On the cross, not only as a deal is done, but as a way that is trod ~ Repairing the world

THE NATURAL ROUTE THROUGH any story is through the experience of its protagonist, and our goal so far has been nothing more ambitious than that: to walk this miserable journey in Jonah's half digested shoes. The curious interpretations that we considered in chapter two, I suppose, tend to emerge when people have pretentiously assumed the Divine perspective, without too much thought about Jonah's or enough humility about their own.[1] But there is another perspective that may help us.

1. Like an angry pet on a chain next to God's throne, barking downwards at the stupid mortals who don't "get it." (One thinks also of the endless beration of the *idiotic disciples!* of the New Testament, who, admittedly lacking two thousand years of theological hindsight, are still not as wise as we who change our minds about everything every five hundred years or so—if Phyllis Tickle is right (Tickle, *The Great Emergence*, 19-31). To "try to get a God's-eye-view of anything, or anyone" says Tom Wright "is a basically promethean—i.e. atheistic—thing" (nomadpodcast.co.uk, interview 85). After all, the Bible was not dictated from heaven, but emerged from the mess of human history, from

Lastly, then, let us re-imagine the story, not through the wearied eyes of the prophet, but from a point of view that probably suits us better: from that of the empire which was confronted as it went about its business as usual. Let's make our home for a moment on the streets of Nineveh, in its market places with its tradesmen, washerwomen and playing children, the coiled beards, the opulence, the beggars and the incense of its cults. Let's observe the brave armies marching in and out in the name of wealth, security, power and greatness, and hear the stories and the talk of victories and losses and the backwardness of those who are resisting the benefits of the empire. From this side of the barbed wire fence we see that the prophetic act, which was incomprehensible to Jonah, was equally incomprehensible to the people on the streets of Nineveh. And perhaps it is in this mutual incomprehension that the act can finally be comprehended.

We return to that moment, the apocalyptic paradigm shift and its awkward silence; the moment just after the gastrically bleached Jewish madman finishes his summarily brief discourse on Assyrian politics and militarism from on top of an empty crate by some fierce looking monument in our great City of Fishes. And there in that awkward silence, although the sun continues its imperceptibly steady route through the sky above them, it seems that time has stopped. And indeed, imperial time *has* stopped.

Something has just happened that it has no category for, and there, on that street corner at least, it cannot continue.[2] It cannot

the pens of people who had no idea they were writing a holy book, and out the lives of people who wouldn't have thought themselves appropriate material for that sort of thing. The God of that book seems to think that we understand things best from below. While we all step on each other's faces trying to climb up to heaven God puts on sandals and becomes a human being.

2. To say that imperial time can be stopped is not to speak of something imaginary, of an imaginary stopping of time. It is, rather, imperial time which is imaginary—an apparently all encompassing reality constructed by a collective act of the imagination; a game, if you will. Jonah's audacious act literally stops imperial time just as a streaker literally stops a cricket match until security can bungle him off. For more thoughts here see Mitchell, *Church Gospel and Empire*, 198-200.

account for this event or respond to it without submitting to the truth of a reality beyond its own. Why? We will see.

In the meantime I have a fancy that perhaps the vagrant, the outsider, the imposter to the ceaseless rhythm of Assyrian imperial time, has not noticed that time has stopped. He stands there in terror, feeling the strain of every second pump, pump, pump through his chest, waiting for some cruel hand to take hold of him and some jagged knife to break the skin of his throat. And then slowly he realizes that something strange is happening, and he sees it in the many pairs of Assyrian eyes all fixed on him and all saying to each other, without looking at each other, *"what is he doing here?"* It is as though they have been visited by a dead man. And they have.

We will call this strange, time-stopping act the Jonaic Interruption. It is the interruption of business as usual by presenting oneself—one's actual physical presence—in vulnerability, to the other. This occurrence can be seen in that look in the eyes of the other which says: *what is she doing here?* or *what is he doing here?* or *what are they doing here?* It may be a look of shocked hostility, or perhaps curious surprise, or perhaps even unexpected delight. But it is more than just a marvelous happening in an ancient tale; it is a practice, and in later times, it would become a movement.[3]

---

3. A Jonaic interruption of mythological proportions occurred on Christmas day of 1914 during World War One, in no man's land between English and German soldiers. It was some of the German soldiers who instigated the audacious interruption in the hell of trench warfare by wandering out to see if any of the English would like a game of football. And for a day, imperial time really was stopped. Future interruptions were predictably suppressed from higher up the chain of command. Similarly mythological is the story of St. Francis who decides to subvert a small town's feud with a man-eating wolf by going into the woods at night to meet the beast. While all had assumed that the only answer was to kill it, St Francis arranged for the townsfolk to bring it some steak each day, and the two parties became friends for generations after. See *Little Flowers of Saint Francis*, 70.

In the last hundred years we've seen the non-violent political campaigns of Gandhi which interrupted the British imperial rule of India by organized non-cooperation with the economic and social structures of the empire. In this tradition also lies the Civil Rights Movement which interrupted segregated spaces like buses and lunch counters, which unified black and white Americans in a

When viewed through the eyes of the other, this Jonaic Interruption is suddenly not the act of idealistic madness that it may have seemed. At least, it is only an act of madness insofar as it is an act of faith (which *is* of course a realm of madness as far as some are concerned). But it is faith of this character: faith that, as they say, *another world is possible,* or to put the matter with the frankness of the Biblical prophets, that another world is inevitable.[4] This is faith because that other world is, in Nineveh at least, nowhere to be seen. The Jonaic Interruption is an act of faith, committed to the mere possibility that, in this pause in time, the balance might slip unexpectedly the other way and the Assyrian imperial order might be revealed as the realm of madness and of ridiculous and misguided idealism, and the possibility of another world glimpsed.

But how? And why? What does the Jonaic Interruption do? What is the nature of its peculiar power?

When we note that the Assyrians had no way to comprehend Jonah's act without acknowledging a reality beyond their own imperial world, we do not mean that they were dumbfounded because Jonah introduces the idea of God. In fact he doesn't mention God, although of course a destroyer is implied. It was quite within the grasp of the Assyrian imperial mindset that the world was full of gods who could be invoked in war and such. They didn't really care. When the Assyrians stood at the gates of Jerusalem in Isaiah's day, Rabshakeh their commander says this:

---

march to the center of power, and which kept to a rigorous ethic of enemy-love and forgiveness for their opponents: "If physical death is the price that I must pay to free my white brothers and sisters from a permanent death of the spirit, then nothing can be more redemptive." so said Martin Luther King Jr. Also in this tradition lies the work of Christian Peacemaker teams who still today interrupt the violence of conflict zones by being there and by getting in the way when everybody else is fleeing.

Closer to home, our musical collective, The Army of the Broken Hearted, along with many other art movements today, chose to play outdoor spaces rather than conventional venues, with the aim of interrupting the corporate dominance and social numbness of public spaces in British cities. Art in an art gallery interrupts nothing.

4. To mention a few references: Isaiah 2:2–4, 25:6–8, 65:17–25, Micah 4:1–5, Romans 8:18–13, Revelation 21:1–4.

> "Has any of the gods of the nations delivered his land out of the hand of the king of Assyria? Where are the gods of Hamath and Arpad? Where are the gods of Sepharvaim? Have they delivered Samaria out of my hand? Who among all the gods of these lands have delivered their lands out of my hand, that the Lord should deliver Jerusalem out of my hand?"[5]

He even proposes that the gods themselves are defecting to the Assyrian empire and handing their peoples over to it:

> "Is it without the Lord that I have come up against this land to destroy it? The Lord said to me, go up against this land and destroy it."[6]

The rhetorical invocation of one god against another was entirely within the imperial mindset. It was all part of imperial bravado, and it still is. The particularities of Jewish monotheism were quite lost on the Assyrians; of course everyone liked to talk as though their god was the biggest and the best. That's just how you play the game.

If imperial time was interrupted that day on the streets of Nineveh, I expect it was because of something more profound than Jonah's eight word sermon, which sounds like the reluctant improvisation of a man who was literally hoping to fail. It was not simply more rhetoric about gods and empires that froze Nineveh that day. That is to say, it was not simply in what Jonah said that this unexpected power is found, but rather in his going there and saying it. It was this revelation of the character of God that changed everything: the prophetic act of a man who offers his neck to his enemies in the small hope of redeeming them. This possibility has no place in the Assyrian imperial mindset—nor in any empire.

When Hobbes described social reality as the war of every man against every man, he was not describing a new development but one that goes back, as Walter Wink saw it, to the domestication

---

5. Isaiah 36:18–20.
6. Isaiah 36:10.

of the horse.[7] It is a fundamental article of the faith of empire. So long as everyone is playing the game, human existence can continue, and so long as we're the strongest, we'll be the ones who keep winning. Of course, other strong contenders are to be admired but feared, lest they start winning and we become the losers. But what of those who deny this article of faith: *the war of every man against every man*? What of those who refuse to apply the counter pressure in the universal competition for life? What of those who won't pull their end of the rope? What do we do with these people? A strong competitor may make us the loser, but these rare quislings threaten to collapse the whole game. And what would life be then?

By marching into the heart of the City of Blood, unarmed and alone, and promising the Assyrians that the game is going to end, it is as though Jonah dismisses his own team from the tug of war—armies, allies, battlements and borders—and then hands the Assyrians the other end of the rope. Of course they look stupid: standing there, each holding their share of that flaccidly drooping cord of expired logic. They've been woken up from a dream that all of a sudden seems ridiculous and they can't get back to sleep again. Whilst moments ago there was nothing but huffing and puffing and rope and muscle and blood and sweat and them and us, suddenly all of that is gone. The imperial clock has stopped. They squint in the glare of the world beyond it that has been revealed to them as reality to their juvenile game.

If we may be excused the philosophical verbosity, we might say that Jonah's Interruption *collapses the dialectic*; he short-circuits the argument between enemies by introducing an outer reality: a third kind of power that doesn't play the game, but rather dismantles it. He doesn't really want to do it, as he openly confesses, because he too is addicted to his end of the rope, just as we all are. He too squints in the terrifying light of another world beyond. Faith in the war of every man against every man is more compelling to our instinct for self-preservation than faith in the

---

7. Wink, *The Powers That Be*. 40–42.

God who is, as Jonah complains, "a gracious God, and merciful, slow to anger, and of great kindness."[8]

And so, while the creatures love the games they have spun among themselves and against one another, the creator loves the creatures, even to the exclusion of their games.

———————————

I had not planned for these reflections to lead towards a substantial discussion of Jesus, and particularly not at the end. I didn't want to fall into that predictable rut of pulling Jesus out of the bag at the last post as though he were some sort of triumphal religious punch line, and neither did I want to mangle Jonah's story by inspecting it backwards through a monocle of Christian theologies and reducing it all to mere typology and foreshadows. But how can we avoid the matter now?[9] It seems to be a peculiarity of the Jesus of the Gospels that he practices the Jonaic Interruption almost constantly, and like nobody else. The more one goes looking for it the more one is found scratching one's head wondering what else he does besides. I can't think of any person or character in history or fiction who seemed so completely bent on the Jonaic practice.

Jesus is forever reacting to the social boundaries of any given situation by loudly ignoring them, being apparently far more captivated by the other, whoever it may be, sat on the opposite side of that imaginary wall. He is not *supposed* to speak to the woman at the well, because she is a woman and he is a man, and they are alone, and she is a Samaritan, and he is a Jew, and they are enemies. She even tells him this is not appropriate, but he carries on anyway and they have a marvelous time which goes on for days afterwards.

8. Jonah 4:2.

9. The case I will make is this: it seems to me that this extraordinary act of Jonah has given us a very illuminating way to view the actions of the first century rabbi, rather than the other way around where the Hebrew Bible is carelessly pushed retrospectively though the meat grinder of Christian theology. Some may think I'm mistaken, and that this is exactly what I have done (of course it can't be entirely avoided). Others may wish to uphold the benefits of retrospective theological meat grinding. The hermeneutical debates abound. In any case I think that at least trying to walk through texts forwards, and to understand them on their own terms, pays off in the end.

He is not supposed to have time for Romans and their poorly servants because the Romans are the oppressors, the occupiers and the enemy who are ruling his people with the sword and taxing them to death. He is not supposed to invite himself to dinner with tax collectors because they are traitors who are getting rich at the expense of their own people in collaboration with the Roman occupiers. Indeed his chosen group of twelve somehow includes both a tax collector and a Zealot (a militant patriot), which ought to be an impossible combination. Nor is he supposed to spend a lot of time with sex workers, because who is? Nor is he, or anyone, supposed to speak to the violent, naked, self-harming man whom the social services of the day had decided to keep chained up in a graveyard at a safe distance from reasonable society (an approach which is still popular today), but Jesus and the twelve nearly drown in a storm trying to get over to him. And when they get there the man immediately asks, *what are you doing here?*[10] Jesus is constantly going to the terrible other in search of the image of God.

He also loved to be interrupted, and it was usually women who had the vision to do so.[11] Like the pagan woman who ventured to ask a Jewish rabbi for help. He tests her interruption, asking—if I may paraphrase slightly—*what are you doing here?* To which she responds by saying something like, *I'm not leaving.* And so he allows himself to be amazed by *her* interruption, and sends her off with peace, affirmation and healing. Or again, like the apparently wayward woman who interrupts a dinner party of respectable religious men by proceeding to wash Jesus' feet with her hair. This is as inappropriate as it sounds. He immediately accepts her time-

10. Ched Myers sees in this stormy crossing to the loathed gentile Decapolis (Mark 4:35–5:2) a direct parallel with Jonah's own story. Jesus is asleep in the stern as the waves crash and boat nearly sinks, and the disciples are torn between fear of a watery death *and* anxiety about what awaits them on the wrong side of lake Galilee. See Myers', *"Sea Changes Part 2"* in Ateek, Duaybis and Tobin, *Challenging Empire*, 119-20.

11. The men only did it at night, or in half-hearted ways like enigmatically climbing up a tree and hoping Jesus would notice. If it's true that it's harder for men to cross the boundaries than women, perhaps it is because it tends to be generations of men who have drawn up the boundaries in their own favour.

stopping gesture and so joins her in the interruption. Meanwhile the other guests around the table all sit there with wide eyes saying to each other, *what is she doing here?* He seems to live for these awkward moments with the other.

If someone were to behave this way today they might well be thought of as a purposefully awkward person, a compulsive trickster and a shallow demagogue who gets kicks out of making decent sorts of people look uncomfortable. But Jesus' interruptions are not to be mistaken for the mere ticks of a generically anarchic character. He does do it on purpose, to be sure—he very purposefully deconstructs social boundaries by making himself present to the other—but this is because he perceives these invisible boundaries of unspoken enmity to be the constructs of a damaged and oppressive order.

More still, how can we possibly now see the climax of the Jesus story as anything but an utterly shocking interruption, comparable to Jonah's own journey to the City of Blood. For those who believe, it is the interruption to end all interruptions—or perhaps the interruption to begin all of our interruptions (although this hardly seems fair on Jonah). Long before he gets there, Jesus begins to talk about journeying to the capital to be handed over to the brutal occupiers and killed. This idea makes as much sense to his disciples as a trip to Nineveh did to Jonah.[12]

So he arrives. And who is more lost and confused now than Pontius Pilate the Roman governor, panicking with his limp end of the tug-of-war rope?[13] He stands there in his airy mosaic crusted hall of Roman opulence, stood opposite the uncategorizable Jewish man who is completely and unnervingly present with him, though without anything much to say to him. What does he do

12. And of course all the same condescending language gets leveled at them for failing to understand why this was a good idea.

13. I have a good friend—a film maker—who has a fascination with Jesus films, and he says that this exchange in John's gospel, between Jesus and Pilate, is always the pivotal scene in any film that includes it. This is the moment that directors relish as the moment that will bring the film together. And yet its meaning still seems ambiguous and continues to generate endless discussion among theologians.

with a messiah who won't fight, and who, for all wants and purposes, appears to have given himself up for no discernible crime? How can Caesar plunder kings who don't even have homes, let alone thrones? With what can he threaten a man who has already offered his neck? The economy of imperial force makes no sense in the presence of this person. Pilate asks Him, *what are you doing here?* rephrasing the question six different ways,[14] and all the while, I fancy, burning with the growing sense that this is the question he himself must answer—he who is stood in a palace in another people's land, ruling it by violence for taxation and profit. Jesus explains the paradigm shift: "My kingdom is not of this world [*kosmos,* meaning *order*]. If my kingdom were of this world, my servants would have been fighting."[15] Pilate becomes increasingly agitated, drawing blanks on the thought of an enemy who can't be fought and a world beyond his imperial horizon, or any other truth besides the peace of the Roman sword. *What even is truth?* he asks. What truth is there except that which we, the powers, have constructed? What world is there outside the war of all against all, and the empire that presides over it?

Just as everybody knows that Jonah is the man who was eaten by a whale, everybody knows that Jesus is the man who hung on the cross. The symbol of the cross refers (rather inaccurately) to the manner in which the Romans used to murder Jews and other troublesome subjects, by nailing them to trees in busy public spaces, with a bit of wood nailed onto the trunk, crossways, so the victim could be hammered up on it with arms outstretched. There they would hang on the tree, gradually asphyxiating over half a day or so, while people came and went and thought about the benefits of obedience to the Roman Empire. And it was to this that Jesus went (as thousands of his people had done), for standing before the occupier and giving his summarily brief discourse on Roman

14. Pilate asks him the following: "Are you the King of the Jews? [. . .] What have you done? [. . .] So you are a king? [. . .] Where are you from? [. . .] You will not speak to me? [. . .] Do you not know I have authority to release you and authority to crucify you?"

15. John 18:36.

politics and militarism. The Jonaic Interruption means going to the terrible other in vulnerability. In that pause in imperial time there may be the revolution of repentance, as there was in Nineveh. Or there may not be, and the interrupter may be sacrificed. And here we see the great trauma of the Book of Jonah finally answered— a belated fifth chapter to the tale played out by another—where, even though the prophet's message is not received by the empire, and he is not sat under the tree outside the city, but rather nailed to it, he calls out to God, not in anger, but with a prayer of forgiveness for the very powers that execute him, as they have so many others.

There are no certainties. The act has death written into it, whether it is the little death of humiliation, or the total death of being killed. One must have died to this order to even contemplate it.[16]

When viewed in this way the cross of Jesus takes on a certain meaning. For many Christians the cross has typically been the place where "it is finished."[17] Here sin is forgiven once and for all. Here is a source that we may turn to and be finally made right with God. For others it is not simply an occurrence that affects them but a path that must be trod, as the disciples were told it was. The way of the cross, however, has come to be regarded as the inward process of dying to the world, and of emerging from whatever crookedness of the soul. But to view the cross as a Jonaic Interruption—and a continuation of the maritime prophet's terrible call— is to recognize it as a call to a radical social and political praxis. To see the cross as only an inward process is to enter the belly of the whale without ever going to Nineveh. To see it only as a done

16. If the cross itself may indeed be viewed as a Jonaic Interruption, during which the sun stopped shining, the earth shook and an executioner repented, we may note two interesting things. Firstly that the symbol continues to have the power to interrupt imperial time and to invite the beholder to the better world that is possible, that is coming, and secondly that the symbol has been quite happily co-opted into the cause of crusades, wars, racist nationalism and cloistered flight from any engagement with any other. It is my curious observation that the cross which is co-opted back to its original imperial purposes tends not to have a Jesus on it. It is, it would seem, the presence of the person (or at least his image) that makes the interruption possible.

17. John 19:30.

deal is to never leave home at all. It must ultimately be embraced as a path to be trod through the world, for the sake of the world. "If anyone would come after me," says Jesus, "let him deny himself and take up his cross and follow me."[18] It is to continuing works of interruption that Jesus calls his disciples: to radical acts of enemy-love, to radical declarations of grace and forgiveness, to radical transgressions of social boundaries and radical compassion for total monsters. And it was into this purpose that they were called to baptize others.

If the death-and-resurrection of baptism means anything, it is a declaration of faith in the resurrection of Jesus. And it is the people who have faith in resurrection who hold the greatest threat to the empire, because the imperial power to end life no longer holds the final word for these.[19] Thus the resurrection is a political act against the current order, and the breaking in of the order to come. It is both hope in that concrete future, of a world beyond empire, renewed and at peace, and it is the power to live out that peace now, through radical enemy-love, in a world still subject to empire.[20]

Even so, it has become easy, in many circles, to talk of following Jesus without ever contemplating this kind of action. There is a pattern of faith which hopes only to receive something from

18. Mark 8:34.

19. "Whoever loses his life for my sake and the gospel's will save it." Mark 8:35.

20. "Do you not know that all of us who have been baptized into Christ Jesus were baptized into his death, in order that, just as Christ was raised from the dead by the glory of the Father, we too might walk in newness of life? For if we have been united with him in a death like his, we shall certainly be united with him in a resurrection like his." So says the apostle Paul (Romans 6:3-5). In seeing Jonah's three days and nights in the belly of the whale as an image of baptism, perhaps we might also see a further resonance with the meaning of his name, *Dove*. Just as the dove brings the first shoots of new life after the flood (which the apostle Peter takes to be a symbol of baptism), and just as Jesus emerges from his own baptism to find the Holy Spirit alighting on him like a dove, perhaps in Jonah also we are to see the dove emerging from that watery baptism in the great fish with the power to renew even the darkest corner of the world, albeit through suffering and gritted teeth.

Jesus which is to be buried until it can be cashed in later, or at best, offered to others as a religious insurance scheme. Just as it is absurd to berate Jonah for complaining about his horrifying trip to Nineveh without ever dreaming of going to visit the militants of Mosul ourselves, it is absurd to talk of following Jesus without ever making the journey to our enemy's door. If we are to speak of following Jesus, we must follow him as he follows on from Jonah: into the space of the enemy and the other.

I recall a friend from the synagogue telling me recently that the Jewish aim was what he called *tikkun olam,* which means "to repair the world." We are called, he said, to the repairing of the world, and so I suppose we are also called against the work of "those who destroy the earth,"[21] to interrupt such work, creating awkward pauses in time in which repentance becomes possible and another world imaginable.

One day there will be an interruption, and imperial time will stop, as it has done many times before, and everyone will wait for it to start up again, but it won't. It finally won't be able to fool itself into being anymore, and all its machinery will be hammered into something good and beautiful, or thrown onto the fire. And then we will know that the world to come is finally here.

21. Revelation 18:11.

Epilogue

"I lay my hand on my mouth. I have spoken once and I will not answer twice."

—JOB

"THE DRAMA'S DONE!" AS Melville wrote, and yet its crisis still hangs gaping before us. And the prophet himself, *the Dove* and *the Sufferer*, shrewdly disappears from his own tale into obscurity and speculation, even as it concludes. The words on the page run out and we are left alone.

Now, even the prophet's alleged tomb is only a dusty ruin in Mosul, where he used to be remembered and revered by the Muslims of that city and by the present-day Assyrians - who are none other than the descendants of "that great city." In recent times the Assyrians have become known by the Arabic letter for "N" with which the militants of the Islamic State war machine have branded them: "N" for Nazarene. It is quite fitting that Jonah's Ninevites were among the first to embrace the gospel of love for the terrible other, and so became devotees of both our Great Interrupters. Now the survivors are displaced, the prophet's shrine is dust, and the City of Blood is ruled by wicked men once again. Do we dare risk the thought that perhaps the descendants of this bloody and disastrous caliphate might one day love and revere the legends, memories and shrines of those who once walked through their gates in search of the image of God, and who paved the way to resurrection for a people locked in a vortex of death?

If anyone is shocked or alarmed at the story we have here retold, then let us hear no more of the cheap, patronizing, and trivializing dismissals of Jonah, as though he were some misbehaving child. Let us hear no more of the racist religious rhetoric about Jonah's alleged religious racism. And let us have no more of the pious sophistry that manages to avoid Jonah's terrible call by reducing it to a metaphor for some theological abstraction or other. Let us rather, together with Job, put hand over mouth and be struck dumb by the prophet's incomprehensible journey into the epicenter of doom, and by the self-emptying love of the God of Jesus Christ. Only when we are shocked, horrified, and unmade by the story of Jonah can we begin to imagine that we have understood it. Only by following him into the whale's belly, by earnestly undergoing the death-and-resurrection of his baptism, and by allowing ourselves also to be unmade and dismantled, dislodged from the structures and obligations of the current order, and empowered with a strength to love that goes beyond ourselves, only then can we begin to adopt the Jonaic practice, the way of the cross and the call of the gospel: to go to the terrible other in search of the image of God.

Perhaps the Book of Jonah ought to be read as Myers reads Mark—cyclically[1]—since it ends as it begins, with God and Jonah together in disagreement. Perhaps the story's refusal to land their dispute is an invitation to the reader—not to put the book down with some self-righteous remark about the disobedience of Jonah—but rather to start the story over, to be troubled by the weight of its call, to face up to our own resistance to it, and to watch and pray and discern what the politics of enemy-love demand of us now, in the time and place in which we stand.

And so, I suppose I will pick up where I left off with my musical, if I may call it that; to the telling and retelling of this strange ballad, in the hope that we ourselves might be interrupted by it.

---

1. See Myers, *Binding the Strong Man*, 399.

Bibliography

Allen. Leslie C. *The Books of Joel, Obadiah, Jonah and Micah*. London: Hodder & Stoughton, 1976.

Ateek, Naim, Cedar Duaybis and Maurine Tobin, eds. *Challenging Empire: God, Faithfulness and Resistance*. Jerusalem: Sabeel Ecumenical Centre, 2012.

Barker, Kenneth L. ed. *The NIV Study Bible*. London: Hodder & Stoughton, 2003.

Brewin, Kester. *Mutiny! Why We Love Pirates and How They Can Save Us*. Vaux, 2012.

Cavanaugh, William T. *Theopolitical Imagination*. London: Bloomsbury T & T Clark, 2013.

Collodi, Carlo. *The Adventures of Pinocchio*. Translated by Ann Lawson Lucas. Oxford: Oxford University Press, 1996.

Calvin, John. *Commentaries, Volume XIV*. Translated by Rev. John Owen. Grand Rapids, Michigan: Baker, 1993.

Eusebius, *The History of the Church*. Translated by G. A. Williamson. London: Penguin, 1967.

Foucault, Michel. *Society Must Be Defended: Lectures at the College de France, 1975–76*. Translated by David Macey. London: Penguin, 2004.

Goetz, Philip W. ed. *The New Encyclopaedia Britannica, 15th Edition: Micropaedia, Vol 6*. Encyclopaedia Britannica, Inc, 2002.

Hegedus, Timothy Michael, *Jerome's commentary on Jonah: Translation with introduction and critical notes* (1991). *Theses and Dissertations (Comprehensive)*. Paper 115. http://scholars.wlu.ca/etd/115

Heisler, Jeanne Marie. *Gnat or Apostolic Bee: A Translation and Commentary on Theodoret's Commentary on Jonah* (2006). *Electronic Theses, Treatises and Dissertations*. Paper 4147. http://diginole.lib.fsu.edu/etd/4147

Hobbes, Thomas. *Leviathan*. Cambridge: Cambridge University Press, 1997.

Jung, Carl Gustav. *Four Archetypes*. Translated by R. C. F. Hull. London: Routledge, 2006.

Kipling, Rudyard. *Just So Stories*. London: Penguin, 1989.

Limburg, James. *Jonah: A Commentary*. London: SCM, 1993.

The Little Flowers of St Francis. Translated by L. Sherley-Price. Harmondsworth: Penguin, 1959.

Martin, Hugh. *Jonah*. Edinburgh: Banner of Truth, 1978.

Melville, Herman. *Moby Dick*. Ware: Wordsworth, 1992.

Mitchell, Roger Haydon. *Church, Gospel & Empire*. Eugene, Oregon: Wipf & Stock, 2011.

Myers, Ched. *Binding the Strong Man: Twentieth Anniversary Edition*. Maryknoll, New York: Orbis, 2014.

Orwell, George. *Inside the Whale and Other Essays*. London: Penguin, 1969.

Pascal, Blaise. *Pensées*. Translated by A. J. Krailsheimer. London: Penguin, 1995.

Suha, Rassam. *Christianity in Iraq*. Leominster: Gracewing, 2006.

Sanders, E. P. *Jesus and Judaism*. Philadelphia: Fortress, 1986.

Schaeffer, Francis. *The God Who is There*. London: Hodder and Stoughton, 1970.

Theodoret. *Ecclesiastical History*. Translated by Rev. Blomfeild Jackson, MA. Whitefish, Montana: Kessinger, 2004.

Tickle, Phyllis. *The Great Emergence*. Grand Rapids, Michigan: Baker, 2009.

Wink, Walter. *The Powers That Be*. New York: Galilee Doubleday, 1999.

Lightning Source UK Ltd.
Milton Keynes UK
UKOW06f1239240716

279063UK00001B/13/P